The Pastoral Nature of Theology

The Pastoral Nature of Theology

Theology

An Upholding Presence

R. John Elford

CASSELL

Cassell
Wellington House, 125 Strand, London WC2R 0BB
370 Lexington Avenue, New York, NY 10017–6550

www.cassell.co.uk

First published 1999

British Library Cataloguing-in-Publication Data
A catalogue record for this book is available from the British Library.

ISBN 0–264–67489–0 (hardback)

ISBN 0–264–67490–1 (paperback)

Typeset by York House Typographic Ltd, London
Printed and bound in Great Britain by T.J. International, Padstow, Cornwall

Contents

For my wife Anne

Acknowledgements

The dedication of this book to my wife Anne is a small but sincere appreciation for her long support of my ministry and academic work and, in particular, for accepting the demands on my time both have made over the years.

The exercise of a Christian pastoral ministry is one of life's great privileges. It has given me a profound experience of the ordinary ways in which we all encounter the joys, frustrations and sorrows of the human lot. In all this, I value beyond measure the blessings and inspiration I have received from others whilst, ostensibly, ministering to them.

Throughout my professional life, I have been blessed with the good company of fellow ministers and academics and I am indebted to them all beyond measure. Professor Ronald Preston has been a support throughout, as well as in the preparation of this volume. I am also indebted to Ian Markham, the Liverpool Professor of Theology and Public Life, for his encouragement, guidance and intellectual energy. Two other theological colleagues at Liverpool Hope University College have also assisted with their specialist knowledge: Dr Kenneth Newport in biblical theology and Mr Tinu Ruparell in the philosophy of religions. I am also grateful to Mr Alfred Westwell, who has been generally obliging and tireless in reading the proofs, and to Mr Christopher Williams for help with the footnotes and indexes. Any remaining shortcomings are, of course, my own responsibility. To all these and many more I express my sincere thanks for sharing the pleasures of the intellectual life and for friendship.

I am grateful to the Editor of *The Expository Times* for permission to reproduce, in a revised form, material in Chapter 2 and to David Higham Associates for permission to print 'Ten types of hospital visitor' by Charles Causley. I am also grateful to my senior colleague at Liverpool Hope,

Professor Simon Lee, for granting me partial secondment from administrative responsibilities to complete this and other books. With colleagues, I am also indebted to him for supporting recent developments in the study of Theology in the College and thereby fulfilling the long-held ambitions of his predecessor and the College Trustees.

Liverpool Hope University College
Easter 1999

Preface

In his poem 'Ten types of hospital visitor', the Cornish poet Charles Causley casts an all seeing eye over the identity and behaviour of hospital visitors.[1] The poem shows Causley's remarkable poetic ability to illuminate the commonplace. It is, moreover, an eye which is particularly observant of the pastoral needs and sensitivities of the hospital patient. Only one of the visitors comes close to meeting these; the sixth.

> The sixth visitor says little,
> Breathes reassurance,
> Smiles securely.
> Carries no black passport of grapes
> And visa of chocolate. Has a clutch
> Of clean washing.
>
> Unobtrusively stows it
> In the locker; searches out more.
> Talks quietly to the Sister
> Out of sight, out of earshot, of the patient.
> Arrives punctually as a tide.
> Does not stay the whole hour.
>
> Even when she has gone
> The patient seems to sense her there:
> An upholding
> Presence.

Of the remaining nine visitors one is chillingly never mentioned. Causley's writing of the sixth visitor provides us with a beautiful and eloquently

concise introduction to the theme of this book. It shows how downright
ordinary and practical the really effective care of one person for another
often needs to be; an upholding presence. It exposes the pretentiousness,
the awkwardness, and the mistaken well-meaningness of so many of the
alternatives. Like poetry at its best, once read, this changes one's perceptions forever, and perhaps not only of hospital visiting.

This book explores the way in which the historical and cultural setting of
theology has a seminal influence on its nature. More specifically, this will
show that the setting is invariably a 'pastoral' one, in the minimal sense of
ordinary care for people, as illustrated by Charles Causley. We will see how
theology always has and still does arise *out* of pastoral concern. In doing so,
we will challenge all those writers on the subject who presume that the
reverse is the case; that pastoral care arises out of theology. This, as we shall
see mistaken, view has led to the widespread further assumption that
pastoral theology is 'applied' theology. Perhaps such a simple mistake has
an equally simple provenance. Most writers on pastoral theology and
pastoral ministers come to pastoral concerns when they are confronted by
them *after* they have studied theology formally. This was certainly my own
experience. Soon after I began formal theological study, at pre-theological
college and then at a theological college and universities, I came to believe
that it was necessary, in the first instance, to focus on what we might call the
ultimate questions of theology in the expectation that once these became
clearer all else would fall into place. Naturally, such questions were about
the possibility and manner of God's existence, his relationship to the world
and about the nature and purpose of such knowledge as we could have of
those things, in the light of the best available philosophical framework one
could find. More specifically, my interest was focused on what it meant to
say that such knowledge as we could have of these ultimate things was either
true or false. After enjoyable and immensely rewarding years of such
theological study, the everyday work of ministry properly intruded and this
brought with it other concerns which became a new focus of continued
theological interest. It was this, in turn, which became the source of a radical
rethink about the relationship of pastoral care to theology. This book is one
result of that.

To start with, the great debates about the ultimate questions of theology
and philosophy seemed remote from and had apparently little to do with the
everyday concerns of ordinary folk. The sick and the bereaved, the men's
group and the youth group knew nothing of Kant's strictures against the use
of 'existence' as a predicate and, even if I had been foolish enough to point

them out to them, they would have cared even less! Here was a different world from the one I briefly had the privilege of studying. The ultimate questions of theology seemed remote from it, important though they were to remain in the background. Life now was concerned with the *penultimate*, with thinking and praying about the joys and sorrows, the sufferings and confusions and often the sheer stupidities of the common lot which are so much a feature of all our lives. Far from being complete, theological enquiries had to begin all over again by paying attention to much more earthy stuff. In circumstances which were to be heightened by his own later tribulations and tragic death to which they led, Dietrich Bonhoeffer wrote similarly of the relationship of the penultimate and the ultimate theological agendas.

> let us ask why it is that precisely in thoroughly grave situations, for
> instance when I am with someone who has suffered a bereavement, I
> often decide to adopt a 'penultimate' attitude, particularly when I am
> dealing with Christians, remaining silent as a sign that I share in the
> bereaved man's helplessness in the face of such a grievous event, and
> not speaking of the biblical words of comfort which are, in fact, known
> to me and available to me.[2]

The penultimate here, as Bonhoeffer explained, 'embraces the whole domain of Christian social life, and especially the whole range of Christian pastoral activity'.[3] Those with any sensitivity to the everyday needs of the human spirit will understand this well. The sheer extent and complexity of those needs, as those in ministry among others are privileged to know, are awesome. Any theology which turns from the ultimate to the penultimate (so understood) to address them has much to do. So much that the task can never be completed.

In the years which followed, all the issues encountered in the everyday work of ministry had one thing in common. A thing which was so obvious and commonplace that it scarcely seemed worthy of attention. That was that the real and pressing, the *penultimate*, questions were all about human well-being both individually and collectively. Unlike ultimate questions, these were ones which arose out of the actual circumstances of people's lives, lives for which as a pastor one had some responsibility to greater or lesser degree. These questions had to be handled differently. They required a total commitment not only of one's intellectual life, but more importantly of one's practical concerns, spirituality and prayer. Here were questions which had to be lived and wrestled with. They were too many, even in parishes in a remote united country benefice, for one person, or even a team of clergy, to cope with. New ways had be found of facing and trying to answer them.[4] Enough of the personal detail, but necessarily enough to illustrate why what follows is like it is, for better or worse.

What sort of questions were these? Could they be categorized? As we have seen, they were all questions about human welfare. Could it, then, be that they were *ethical* questions? Ethical dilemmas were certainly common among them, in the clear sense that they were so often preoccupied with what people should or should not do. But there was more to it than that. These were different questions about what people felt, whether they cried or not, and about how they related to each other, often in the most personal of circumstances. For the spiritually inclined they were also, for these reasons, questions about how they prayed. Ethical questions were partly what they were about, but that was all. There was more to them. The only category which could embrace them all was 'the pastoral'. They had to do with *care* in every sense. The care of people for each other, in great things and in small, collectively as well as individually. Little wonder then that, in the Christian tradition, the phrase 'the cure of souls' has been used persistently to describe this by writers from many different traditions. The definition, or rather the relocation, of the pastoral in the Christian tradition is, therefore, what this book is about. As we shall see, ethical questions permeate pastoral ones but, as such, they are better understood as a sub-set of something wider – the pastoral itself. More radically, as we shall see, the pastoral is not only embracing of the ethical, it is embracing of all theology in the Judaeo-Christian tradition. Only, we shall argue, when it is seen as such can it be understood for what it profoundly is in that tradition, and only then can the other riches of that tradition be put in their proper context. All this will challenge widespread assumptions that the pastoral is something at the periphery of that tradition, or something which only concerns its 'application'. Chapter 1 will explain why this is the case.

Before we turn to that, however, there is an important caution to be noted by way of introduction. It will have to be referred to throughout, but it is so important that it is deserving of mention here. It concerns the obviously *interdisciplinary* nature of pastoral theology and care. Pastoral issues and problems are so diverse in their content and wide-reaching in their consequences that they of necessity straddle the distinctions between discrete academic disciplines. There might have been a time in the not too distant past when this was thought, by some, to be reason enough to consider any neous and ordinary exercise of pastoral care by the unlearned and that conducted by those who have received some form of appropriate training for it. It is equally important to understand the relationship between the two.

A death occurs. The bereaved are grief-stricken to silence. A pastorally qualified minister arrives who is fully conversant with the literature on grief analysis and on how to apply it to actual situations.[10] The pastor notices some beautifully and simply arranged wild flowers. They are so fresh that they must have been picked since the death occurred and brought by someone, since the bereaved had not left the house. The flowers are the centre of attention, a real expression of a neighbour's care, possibly more effective than the words in such circumstances which are invariably so difficult. Such simple actions may need to be followed by other things, but nothing can obscure or deny their importance. This is why a great deal of the literature of pastoral studies has been á literature about how to do things. This will always remain an important aspect of pastoral studies. Paying minute attention to the practical detail of simple actions is always necessary if the cared-for are to receive the best of attention.

These introductory remarks serve to remind us at the outset that the 'pastoral' is, at the very least, something of a 'catch all' for a wide range of important human activity. Without wanting to attempt a final definition, I propose, for the purpose of this book, that the 'pastoral' should be linked to care, a care that expresses itself both individually and/or corporately.

Pastoral theology is, then, the study of the nature and purpose of pastoral attitudes and actions under God. It seeks: to identify such actions; to show what it means to call them pastoral; and to explore the theological resources upon which this meaning draws. It asks whether or not there are pastoral attitudes and actions, or aspects of them, which can be described as Christian. An important part of this study, as we shall see throughout, is the examination of ways in which contemporary pastoral attitudes and actions draw on older Christian thought and practice. This is now necessary because secular pastoral insight has become so generally advanced in the twentieth century that some think it supplants all that has gone before. Making this point in an important article, Tom Oden claimed that Christian pastoral care had 'lost its identity'. He writes,

A major effort is needed today to rediscover and re-mine the classical models of Christian pastoral care, and to bring back into availability the key texts following about fifty years of neglect, a neglect the depths of which are arguably unprecedented in any Christian century.[11]

We will examine this claim in Chapter 3 and see that there is much to commend it. In Chapter 2 we will consider why pastoral theology raises fundamental questions about our views of human nature.

Another issue which makes pastoral theology, like the pastoral itself, also difficult to define concerns the range of subjects it has to address. This is the reason why pastoral theology is sometimes looked upon with suspicion by specialists in other disciplines. This charge of 'generalism' is a very real one, and the suspicion that there is some truth in it has done much to impede the establishment of pastoral theology as an academic discipline alongside others.

We have already considered what it means to say that pastoral theology, like some other areas of study, may be described as *interdisciplinary*. Such studies are now proliferating in reaction to the increasing specialization of much advanced contemporary study. Specialisms are necessary and with the inexorable increase in human knowledge they will remain so. But they create many obstacles. Language is just one of them. The more specialized a study becomes, the more necessary it invariably is for it to develop its own technical language.

Difficulties such as these are now widely recognized, with the result that many believe that the advancement of their own specialisms will increasingly depend upon an ability to engage with those of others. Actual problems, after all, are seldom so obliging as to organize themselves into specialisms! In this context, 'pastoral theology' may find a more congenial academic atmosphere in which to establish its credentials than it has formerly done. Important new opportunities will begin to emerge and it will be less imperative to ask what pastoral theology is, in the expectation that a definition could be found which would make it a specialism among others. We are likely to make more progress with our understanding of pastoral theology by not seeking such a definition at all beyond the general one given above and concentrate, rather, on exploring this through a broader and interdisciplinary account of its nature.

Pastoral theology and traditional theology

Pastoral theology, in its modern form, is a comparatively new arrival in British universities, although 'practical theology' as it is called in Scottish universities has a much older pedigree and in the United States much of it is found in writings on psychological and social issues. In Britain, at least, pastoral theologians find themselves working alongside colleagues in the longer established theological disciplines such as biblical studies, ecclesiastical history, doctrine, the philosophy of religion, comparative religion, languages and so on. In some places, at the Universities of Manchester and Edinburgh, for example, pastoral theology is twinned with the study of Christian ethics and some members of staff have been expected to research and teach both subjects.[12] In the light of all this, an obvious way of describing pastoral theology is to say that it is 'applied' theology, in the sense that some sciences, for example, physics and mathematics, exist in 'pure' and 'applied' forms. There are some attractions to such a view. The so-called 'applied' disciplines do not threaten the integrity of their 'pure' antecedents. Moreover, the precedence of the 'pure' disciplines suits an arrangement in which their application is a subsequent and separable enterprise. The use of this pure/applied distinction to explain the relationship of theology to pastoral theology often lies behind the view that it is not possible to undertake the formal study of pastoral theology without first obtaining some grounding in more traditional theological studies, making it, therefore, more suited to postgraduate levels of study.

There may, furthermore, be evidence that the pure/applied distinction in Christian theology is to be found in Christian tradition itself. It is possible to identify in a number of places in the New Testament, for example, separable emphases on the proclamation of the gospel on the one hand and on the working out of its pastoral and practical implications on the other. The writings of St Paul contain numerous examples of this. In the epistle to the Romans, for example, a clear division occurs between the exposition of the gospel in chapters 1–12 and the consideration of its implications throughout the remainder of the epistle. Paul can, indeed, be seen as a preacher *and* a pastor, and one, moreover, who studies pastoral problems in detail by giving them his specific and often sustained attention. We will consider more fully the significance of the writings of St Paul for pastoral theology in Chapter 3.

These and other reasons for supposing pastoral theology to be 'applied' theology make the suggestion so attractive that it might seem possible to proceed without further ado. To do so would, however, be seriously mistaken. To understand why, we first need to consider an important feature of Christian theology.

The view that Christian theology cannot exist in a 'pure' form as though it were somehow independent of its social settings and applications has become increasingly recognized. Examples can be found in ways in which Christian communities, especially in Asia and Latin America, have asserted their independence from the dominant theological influences of Rome, Europe and North America. The broadly Hellenic thought forms of Western theology have been and are increasingly challenged by theologies which are created by and for specific communities, for which the categories of Western theology either have no meaning or are suspected as being the coded means whereby the Northern Hemispheric cultures maintain their control of and influence over other ones. The upshot of this is that theology is now increasingly done in different ways and for different purposes in different places. In a recent study of some of the implications of this, Robert J. Schreiter points out that:

> There has been an important shift in perspective in theology in recent years. While the basic purpose of theological reflection has remained the same – namely, the reflection of Christians upon the Gospel in the light of their own circumstances – much more attention is now being paid to how those circumstances shape and respond to the Gospel.[13]

He goes on to claim that the real task of theology is to create within a wider context 'local theologies' which bring the liberating power of the gospel to bear on the actual circumstances of people's lives. These theologies may also be called 'indigenous' theologies. They begin with a refusal to accept the imposition of a theological agenda on a particular place or circumstance, regardless of what such places and circumstances may require. The concern which is commonly held to be important for the formation of theology understood in this way, is that of political oppression and its corollary, economic exploitation. This appears in different ways in different places and, for that reason, the theological responses to these phenomena have to be culture-specific. To achieve this, they begin by rejecting any views which claim explicitly or implicitly that there can be only one theological agenda which is preconceived, set for all time and universally valid.

The theologies which have been produced to respond to these needs have, not surprisingly, been called 'liberation' theologies and they have had such popular appeal that they have enabled the cultures in which they emerge to assert their theological independence from often overpowering external influences. Such liberation theologies may be short-lived and be superseded by other theologies as perceptions of social need change. For this reason they may be described as 'contingent' or 'contextual' theologies.

They do not, of course, always eschew all that comes from elsewhere, but they do subject what does so to critical analysis and, if then thought necessary, to revision. This process has created widespread quests for new understandings of theological authority and, in doing so, it has directly challenged many of those who represent older and more widely accepted theological authorities.

Another, and for our purpose important to observe, feature of the liberation theologies is the obvious fact that they have a markedly pastoral nature. They address themselves to actual human needs and consequently often become allied with specific political movements in pursuit, for example, of justice for the oppressed. They often side with the poor in seeking politically and economically realistic ways of doing something about their condition. Such quests for effective action have often been influenced by Marxist political and economic theory. Reasons for this are not hard to find. Marx derived his political and economic theory from his original, pre-1848, philosophy of freedom.[14] This claimed that the circumstances of human bondage were of human making and that, therefore, what human beings had created in the first place they could subsequently change. The implication of this being that, if they fail to effect this change, their present condition is entirely their own responsibility. This makes it imperative to bring about changes by revolution if necessary. As a philosophy of freedom this can scarcely be criticized. Its manifest shortcomings in experiments in Marxist government arise more directly from political failings than they do from the philosophical origins of Marxism itself. Marxist practices and liberation theologies spring from more noble sentiments concerning the desire to raise the consciousness of the oppressed to a level where they feel able to do something about their condition. All this is of the essence of pastoral concern, as we will consider at some length in Chapter 6 when we examine the relationship of pastoral theology to social and political issues.

This brief discussion of liberation theology has made an important point. The proper agenda of theology is not self-setting. It cannot be pre-programmed. This places in very real question the supposition that theology can exist in some pure form without reference to its applications and independently of any considerations of the context in which it is created. This reminds us that theology is done by human beings and, therefore, always reflects directly or indirectly their social and political circumstances as well as their aspirations. This is why the often asked question about the relevance of liberation theologies outside Latin America and Asia is misplaced. The precise circumstances which make it relevant there may not exist elsewhere, where other needs will set other agendas with different theological outcomes. Most obvious current examples of these in the West focus on questions of racial and sexual equality, on the need to control rapidly emerging technologies and on environmental issues. All of these have been the subject of theological attention and revision which is, in many ways, methodologically parallel to what happens in the liberation theologies.

Is liberation theology simply a twentieth-century phenomenon or does it, rather, draw important attention to something which has always been true of theology? And, if so, does this have any significance for the way in which the relationship of theology to pastoral theology and care should be understood? In answer to these questions we will now consider some examples of the most formative theological periods in the Judaeo-Christian tradition and, in doing so, notice that they invariably have one important thing in common. Namely, they show how theology has never, in fact, been done independently of its historic settings, but rather that it has always been influenced by them to such an extent that it mirrors the pastoral features we have observed in liberation theology. That being the case, we will then see that the pure/applied model for understanding the relationship of theology to pastoral theology must be put aside in favour of a much more radical view. The first example we will consider is, and should be, the biblical one, since it would obviously be unwise to draw any conclusions in this respect about the nature of theology in general if they could not be seen to resonate with its biblical roots.

Pastoral care in the biblical tradition

In Chapter 3 we will consider the biblical pastoral traditions in some detail. Here we will do so only to show that pastoral concerns were foremost in the minds of the biblical writers and became the central influence on what they wrote.

The Bible can be read as the historical account of how the Judaeo-Christian tradition developed from the fact that God revealed himself on Sinai and in the life of Jesus, in the sense that there is thought to be a pure givenness of revelation on the one hand and the responses to it on the other. Arguably, this is not correct. The Old Testament, for example, does not contain a pure theology of what is given in revelation and a separate narrative of its consequent application. It contains, rather, a theology which is being continually reworked under the constraints of ever changing historical circumstances. In the earliest period, for example, after the death of Saul (1 Sam 6.14), David rose to power rapidly through a combination of successful military strategy and popular consent (2 Sam 5.12). He soon established the new kingdom with its, hitherto in Israel, unprecedented institutions. He fought off aggression and consolidated his power. As a result, Israel had, for the first time, the trappings of a state, with its headquarters firmly established in Jerusalem. The earthly 'City of David' was born. Historically speaking, these dramatic changes came about remarkably rapidly. Naturally, theological thinking in Israel also had to adapt to the new challenges and opportunities. First, it had to embrace the previously alien notion of kingship. David was crowned king, as Saul had been, but was now king of Judah and Israel. Israel, in effect, adopted an institution which was foreign to its own older and more primitive tribal and nomadic traditions. Since it lacked precedent in Israel, it was patterned on Egyptian and other models. This dramatic achievement was consolidated by Solomon, by which time little remained that was recognizable from the old pre-conquest Israel, apart from the oral traditions about its nomadic past. Even these, however, were being affected by the new social, political and economic circumstances. The central theological problem, however, was that of the monarchy. To some it represented paganism, to others it was evidence of Yahweh's crowning achievement in Israel. These few brief remarks show how Israel's changing social and political circumstances had a direct bearing on its theological understanding, which can be traced throughout the developing Old Testament literature on kingship. The process here is far from one in which an unchanging theology *brings about* social changes. Rather, it is a process in which the social and economic needs of Israel can be seen to be bringing about changes in its theology.

Many other such examples of the social influence on the theology of the Old Testament could be given. The protest of Amos was against the corruption and injustice which had become established in Israel and against the feeling of national supremacy and disregard for the other nations which had become an accepted fact (Amos 3.1). In order to denounce such attitudes, Amos had to explore new theological insights. The most important of these was his stress on the ethical supremacy of Yahweh (Amos 5.15). The need for the exercise of justice and mercy became the predominant theme of his writing, along with a new emphasis on God's judgement. He thereby produced a type of theology which had not existed in Israel before. Here again, we see a pattern of events in which the increasing urbanization of Israel, the rise of exploitative upper classes and the general disregard with which Israel came to hold the other nations, required new types of theological emphasis and insight.

Even more pointed for our purpose, is the prophetic witness of Jeremiah. During the fall of Jerusalem to the Babylonians, King Zedekiah sought a word from Jeremiah when military defeat seemed imminent and inescapable. Jeremiah replied with prophecy which focused on the defeat and subsequent exile and showed how it was part of Yahweh's plan for the nation (Jeremiah 37.17). He later maintained his prophetic work by advising the exiles in Babylon to adapt to the radically changed circumstances in which they found themselves by building houses and living in them. Here again, the development of Israel's central theology was clearly influenced by social circumstances. A consideration of how this process occurs in the New Testament will complete these reflections on how the biblical theology is throughout constantly formed and reformed in response to changing events and the pastoral needs they precipitate.

Jesus proclaimed a radical message about the Kingdom of God and urged his immediate followers to prepare themselves for it. In response, they accepted that the world would soon come to an end and this became the prevailing view in the earliest Christian communities. But the longer that end was delayed, the more necessary it became to change earlier expectations. For this reason the original message of Jesus was changed. The central change, as Bultmann has expressed in a memorable phrase, was that 'the proclaimer became the proclaimed'.[15] Jesus' message of the Kingdom became a message about him and the Kingdom. As the expected return of the Lord did not occur, the more necessary it became for Christian apologists to address the widespread perplexity this caused. What, for example, would happen to those who died in the interim? What was to be done about the ongoing problems of life? Should the divorced remarry? What were Christians to do about property and possessions? What, importantly, were they to teach their children? In response to practical questions such as these, a revised theology emerged which still sustained a belief in the Lord's return but which was also able to countenance its delay. Indeed, by the end of the century the fact that the delay would be indefinite was widely acknowledged. St Luke's Gospel, which arguably dates from this period, accepts the possibility that the second coming of the Lord would be indefinitely delayed. St Luke, therefore, reflects throughout on the significance of a permanent period of history which will intervene and separate the first and the second coming of the Lord.[16] Indeed, at the apex of the Gospel and its sequel the book of Acts, he produces a theology of the ascension which explains the present work of the risen and ascended Lord. The theology of Luke–Acts is a theology which is similar in many respects to the one still widely held in Western theology, namely; that the Lord has appeared, is risen, reigns with God in glory and will return at some unknown time in the future. The seeming permanence of history is, therefore, to be treated with seriousness as the arena in which faith and salvation are to be worked out this side of the Kingdom.

These brief remarks only begin to indicate the complexity of the significance of the delay of the Lord's second coming in early Christianity, but they are sufficient for our purpose. They illustrate how, in the New Testament, ever-changing historical circumstances and ever-changing perceptions of pastoral need, brought about changes in theological understanding.

Changing pastoral needs and theology

It has now become clear from this brief exploration that biblical theology is made up of a mixture of reflection on older traditions in the light of the present. The result is that the traditions become constantly reworked in ways which produce both continuities and discontinuities with what has gone before. The central claim of this book is that reflection on human pastoral need *consistently* plays a seminal role in all this. Nowhere do we find a 'pure' theology which becomes 'applied' in changing circumstances. The content of the theology itself is vulnerable to change through a constant process of reinterpretation and revision in which it is far too simplistic to say the there was ever a 'pure' theology which was imperiously 'applied' to changing circumstances. The relationship between the two was far more complex, interactive and creative. So understood, biblical theology is best seen as an ongoing process. We will later consider the pastoral implications of this.

Can the same be said of the subsequent development of Christian theology? Can its formation also be shown to be influenced by human pastoral need? The following brief consideration of seminal periods in the history of Western Christian theology will, in fact, show this to be precisely the case. We will examine three examples. They are not the only ones which could be chosen, but they are seminal enough to require little justification for their selection.

Augustine

The first example is the theology of St Augustine. He flourished at a crucial period in the development of Western culture and theology. The diminishing Roman empire came to a dramatic end with the fall of Rome to the Goths in 410 c.e. The city of Rome had been the last remaining stronghold of the diminishing and increasingly threatened empire. Its fall precipitated a total collapse of confidence in a way of life which had been centuries in the making.

> Augustine's immediate reaction to this, in a manner which was typical of him, was not just to answer the questions people were asking but to probe behind them to more fundamental issues. What he wanted to do was to wean his people away from putting their faith in inadequate symbols of security.[17]

One suspicion, held by many, was that Rome's demise was the consequence of its adoption of Christianity as its official religion. Rome would have survived, it was argued, if she had relied on the old pagan deities and not the God of Christianity. St Augustine wrote *The City of God* largely out of pastoral concern to answer such fears and suspicions. He argued that the fall of Rome was less horrendous under Christian rule than it would otherwise have been. He further suggested that the demise of Rome as an earthly city should not deter Christians from seeking an unchanging heavenly one, but rather that it should inspire them to do so. 'City' in Augustine's writing is a technical term for something like a 'community of interest', hence the ravaging of a community of earthly interest did not at all imply the same of the heavenly one. Augustine argued that the quest for spiritual truth was a quest of love to God from the earthly city. The love of *eros* reaching upward, only to find its way blocked by its own shortcomings; which Augustine called its 'self-captivation'. This, explained Augustine, is relieved only by the love of God, *agape*, reaching down to create a new love, *caritas*, in which humans are able, regardless of the wretchedness of their lot in the earthly city, to behold their creator in a joy for which they are destined.[18] St Augustine, by this means, created a theology which not only took contemporary social and political circumstances seriously, it also importantly understood them as being the sole reasons why the task of theological reconstruction became imperative.

   The scope of St Augustine's achievement is, of course, more complex and profound than these brief remarks suggest. But the central point is clear. St

Augustine's theological writing and especially *The City of God* was made necessary because of dramatic changes in human circumstances and the pastoral needs they created. If theology was to maintain its credibility at all it could not ignore these needs. In fact, Augustine's theology became so successful in fulfilling its purpose that its influence has remained long after the memory faded of the events which made it so necessary. What he established was that not only could a belief in the unity of God and in the all-pervading purpose of his love be maintained in spite of the fall of Rome, but that such a belief was, in fact, made even more necessary because of it. Once again we see that the pure/applied distinction of theology and pastoral theology is inadequate. The pastoral application is central to the re-formulation of theology itself. So understood, Augustine's work in general, and *The City of God* in particular, stands as a pastoral enterprise of the first rank.

Luther

The second illustration of our theme in Western theology is taken from the writings of Martin Luther. The social and political upheavals which made his theological reconstruction necessary had been long in the making and need little introduction. Northern Europe had been undergoing a long process of intellectual and political self-affirmation. The origins of this lay in the Renaissance, which generated a new sort of anthropocentric learning. This provoked an openness of spirit and enquiry which was from the outset determined to be unfettered by ecclesiastical or other forms of institutional control. This, so-called, new 'humanism' had its own dynamic and was unstoppable. The rapid rise of book production and the consequent dissemination of knowledge at an unprecedented speed, marked, among other things, by the phenomenal spate of university foundations in Northern Europe (there were nine in Germany between 1450 and 1517) gives some indication of the intellectual energy and independence of spirit which was the essence of the period. All this was echoed, little or much, throughout Northern Europe. Such intellectual self-affirmation well suited the concurrent attempts of the Princely states in Northern Europe to assert their own territorial, political and economic independence from Rome. 'It was the aim of the territorial ruler to gain the allegiance of his people with respect to every aspect of their lives: economic, social, political, cultural and religious.'[19] One result of all this was that whole areas of thought and activity were withdrawn from ecclesiastical influence and control. Something we now recognize and describe as the 'secular' was becoming a widespread reality. It might well, as noted, have had other roots but they were all bearing rapid fruit. Whole societies had undergone, in a historically short period of time, a dramatic intellectual as well as political change.

This was the milieu in which Martin Luther created a 'new' theology. He was an Augustinian monk, who drew deeply on the work of his spiritual and intellectual master, St Augustine. In place of Augustine's talk of two 'cities', Luther spoke of two 'kingdoms'. The earthly kingdom, Luther held, was at God's left hand and the heavenly kingdom was at his right. Only God, according to Luther, knows the final truths about the relationship of each to the other. In the earthly kingdom, at God's behest, human life and affairs enjoyed independence and autonomy. This is not, however, complete because God has provided, within the autonomous sphere of the earthly kingdom, 'orders' or 'social institutions' through which his love was ministered to human beings, whether they were aware of it or not. These orders were: work, marriage, the family, and the state. Here, in its essence, was the foundation of a theology which gave the newly established autonomy of human life and thought a theological rationale. It was for this reason widely socially and politically acceptable, particularly to those who were jealous of their new-found intellectual and political freedoms. Since, according to Luther, the saving power of the Word of God could be appropriated *sola fide*, by faith alone, his theology contained such a respect for the autonomy of secular affairs that he became notoriously politically conservative. It held an intense dislike of any area of overlap between the functions of churches and those of states. This accounted, in large measure, for his hatred of social and political rebellion as was demonstrated when he, infamously, instructed the Princes that they should slay the peasant rebels.[20] It is important to notice for our purpose that Luther's theology was produced in response to the perceived needs of a radically and inexorably changing intellectual, social, political and economic situation. He did not, however, break entirely with all his mediaeval roots. Many of them, such as his belief in an albeit qualified mediaeval social order, remained. But the central thrust of his theological genius can only be understood as a pastoral response to the radical changes we have briefly noted. The same was generally true of the work of the other Reformers, the classic example being that of the alleged influence of Calvinism on the modern development of capitalism.[21] Here again the pure/applied distinction between theology and pastoral theology can be seen to be inadequate. Pastoral concern, rather, can once again be seen to be the reason for the development of a new theology.

Barth

The third example of an influential theology which was born out of pastoral need is deliberately chosen from the twentieth century. That need was generated by the First World War and particularly because its horror broke on a European culture which, if it remembered the suffering of war at all, did so only on the comparatively tolerable scale of lesser, localized, and geographically removed conflicts. For Karl Barth, the outbreak of the war was a 'double madness' because it involved both theological and political ineptitude. Barth had received the greater part of his theological education from Adolf von Harnack whose liberal theology stemmed from Schleier-macher. As a result, it drew heavily on human experience and observation and caused Harnack to proclaim with confidence that he considered the truths of theology and science to be as one. This led, above all, to a theology of optimism with an explicit confidence in the inevitable improvement, materially and spiritually, of the human condition. On 1 August 1914 Barth was beginning his intended life's work as a pastor in Safenwil. To his regret he was not enlisted, but he threw himself into the ministry to those who were. The war soon became for him an all-consuming preoccupation, pastorally and intellectually. With horror, he discovered that most of his German theological teachers, including Harnack, were among the ninety-three signatories to the *Manifesto of the Intellectuals*. This identified them as supporting the war policies of Kaiser Wilhelm II. Barth declared that, for him, this was the twilight of the Gods in which all religion and scholarship was changed completely 'into intellectual 42 centimetre cannons'.[22] All these intellectuals, according to Barth, were ethically compromised by the ideology of the war to such an extent that it indicated that 'their exegetical and dogmatic presuppositions could not be in order'.[23] In September 1914 Barth wrote to his colleague E. Thurneysen, a pastor at nearby Leutwil,

> The formula 'God does not will the War' is perhaps misleading. God does not will egotism, but He does will that egotism should reveal itself in war and become itself the judgement. Thus, the will of God to judge is nothing other than love, the revelation of the divine righteousness. I would relate the wrath of God yet more strongly to the 'Godless existence' itself and would think of social injustice and war as symptoms or consequences of the latter.[24]

By the summer of 1916 the theological problem was clear to Barth. During an evening visit to Leutwil, his friend Thurneysen prompted him to see that what was needed was a preaching, instruction and pastoral care which was based on a 'wholly other' theological foundation. Barth and Thurneysen returned again to the study of fundamentals which for them meant biblical theology, and especially St Paul's letter to the Romans. Barth writes:

> I sat under an apple tree and began to apply myself to Romans with all the resources that were available to me at the time . . . I began to read it as though I had never read it before. I wrote down carefully what I discovered, point by point. I read and read and wrote and wrote.[25]

What Barth discovered was that 'the collapse of our cause must demonstrate once and for all that God's call is exclusively his own. This is where we stand today.'[26] Barth concluded that God cannot be reduced to, or appropriated by, human interests and activities. All humans stood under God's judgement. The failure of the recent past had been a failure to remember this fundamental truth and the future could only be reconstructed if it were re-learned and applied. The result was that Barth's developing career soon led him away from the pastorate to Göttingen as Professor of Theology. There he came to see that the task of theology and preaching were the same 'the taking up and passing on the word of God'. The Word of God could only be understood if it was seen for what it was: a word which was dialectically opposed to the word of man. With this insight 'dialectical theology' was born. It soon attracted the attention and labours of a whole generation of rising theologians up to and including the present. In this way Barth, Thurneysen and their successors created a theology which spoke to, rather than was compromised by, the dramatic, widespread and overwhelming suffering the war generated.

The pattern here is now a familiar one, echoing what we observed in the work of Augustine and Luther. A pastoral crisis calls received theological wisdom into question, especially when that wisdom (as it was for Barth) is suspected of contributing to the crisis itself. Theology then has to be reconstructed anew for pastoral reasons. A new integrity has to be sought which is resonant with the most profound contemporary insights into human need and suffering, as it is manifested not only in the lives of individuals, but also in the behaviour and needs of whole societies.

The point of discussing Scripture, Augustine, Luther and Barth in this way, has been to show that it is totally mistaken to believe that theology exists in separable 'pure' and 'applied' forms. Rather, the pastoral relevance of theology is what makes its existence necessary in the first place. It is, as we should always remember, done by human beings for their own sake. This is why it speaks to them most profoundly and creatively when it addresses the actual circumstances in which they find themselves, especially when they feel threatened and insecure. The conclusion of all this is clear. Pastoral need, concern and action are what prompt theology and make it necessary. This means that when we study the theology of pastoral care, we are not studying an adjunct to theology. To study the theology of pastoral care is, in fact, to study the origin of theology itself. Indeed, this simple insight may well go some way to enabling us to study the history of theology afresh, and in so doing help us to see that theology is part of a wider and ongoing endeavour in which human beings reflect on the nature of their ever changing lot before a righteous God.

To claim this is not to deny that, once it is started in this way, the study of theology should not develop its various technical specialisms. But we are clearly mistaken if we become so impressed by such specialisms, and the professional way in which they are invariably organized and exercised, that we suppose that they constitute the proper stuff of theology. Such specialisms are, rather, the service facilities provided by professionals for the benefit of all whose task it is to do theology in its living pastoral tradition. They become in turn, not optional adjuncts to theological study, but are rather the necessary conditions of it. Without them, theological study is ever in danger of becoming ill-informed and, doubtless, misdirected. But the point of this discussion has been to show that there is a prior and inseparable human pastoral dimension to the creation of theology. This is why it demands the study of anthropology and study of the welfare of human beings in the widest sense.

Put another way, it is has been argued that theology should be understood as *praxis*, using that now overworked word to mean something like 'reflective action'. Its use is meant to avoid the trap of thinking that 'theory' and 'practice' are always separable constructs. Under the influence of Aristotle, Western culture has traditionally separated practice from theory. But more recently, under the more modern influence of Hegel and Marx in particular, *praxis* has been understood as something like reflection in action. Robert Schreiter, again, has argued that to describe theology as *praxis* means that it has three tasks: (i) to distinguish true from false consciousness, (ii) to enable continuing reflection, (iii) to sustain the transfiguring theological activity.[27] Examples of the sort of theology which Schreiter and others are calling attention to, as we have seen in this discussion, can be found in the liberation

theologies of South America and Asia. But this should not lead us mistakenly to suppose that theology and practice, so understood, only has a
meaning and application in such extreme and contemporary political and
economic conditions. It has always applied whenever theological reconstruction has been undertaken, particularly in its historically formative
periods. This is central to our understanding of the pastoral nature of all
theology.

So, this chapter concludes where we started. Pastoral theology is not a
branch of Christian theology; it essentially (*sic*) is Christian theology. Nor is
it a professional activity for a minority who are called, trained or appointed.
Instead, it is the activity which lies at the heart of the Christian life for all. It
focuses on the 'personal' and on the deepest needs people experience both
individually and collectively. For this reason we must now turn to a consideration of how Christians and others have understood the term in the
recent past.

Notes

1   Butler, J. (1726) *Fifteen Sermons ii.* London.
2   See Campbell, A. V. (1985) *Paid to Care, The Limits of Professionalism in Pastoral Care*, London: SPCK.
3   Clebsch, William A. and Jaekle, Charles R. (1975) *Pastoral Care in a Historical Perspective*, p. 13. New York: Aronson.
4   Pattinson, Stephen (1993, second edition) *A Critique of Pastoral Care*, p. 18. London: SCM.
5   Carr, Wesley (1997) *Handbook of Pastoral Studies*, p. 9. London: SPCK.
6   Wilson, H. S. *et al.* (1996) *Pastoral Theology from a Global Perspective*, New York.
7   Graham, Elaine (1996) *Transforming Practice: Pastoral Theology in an Age of Uncertainty*, p. 3. London: Mowbray.
8   Ibid., p. 7.
9   Ballard, Paul and Pritchard, John (1996) *Practical Theology in Action*, London: SPCK.
10 E.g. Spiegel, Yorik (1977) *The Grief Process*, London: SCM.
11 Oden, T. C. (March 1980) 'Recovering lost identity'. *The Journal of Pastoral Care*, vol. XXXIV, no. 1, pp. 4–19.
12 See Elford, John (1983) 'Pastoral studies in the University of Manchester', *Contact*, 80, pp. 27–30.
13 Schreiter, R. J. (1985) *Constructing Local Theologies*, p. 1. London: SCM.
14 See Kamenka, Eugene (1974) 'Marxism and ethics', in Hudson, W. D., ed. (1974) *New Studies in Ethics*, vol. 2, pp. 289–360. London: Macmillan.
15 Bultmann, R. (1962) *Theology of the New Testament*, vol. 2, p. 33. London: SCM.

16 See Conzelmann, L. (1960) *The Theology of St. Luke*, London: Faber & Faber.
17 Rowe, T. (1974) *St. Augustine*, p. 110. London: Epworth.
18 See Nygren, A. (1953) *Agape and Eros*, p. 501. London: SPCK.
19 Grimm, H. J. (1973) *The Reformation Era: 1500–1650* (second edition), p. 16. London: Macmillan.
20 Luther, M. (1967) 'Against the robbing and murdering hordes of peasants', *Luther's Works*, vol. 46, pp. 49–55. Philadelphia: Fortress Press.
21 See Weber, M. (1930) *The Protestant Ethic and the Spirit of Capitalism*. London: Allen & Unwin.
22 Busch, E. (1976) *Karl Barth*, p. 81. London: SCM.
23 Ibid.
24 tr. Smart, James D. (1964) *Revolutionary Theology in the Making*, p. 21. London: Epworth.
25 Busch, *Karl Barth*, pp. 98–9.
26 Ibid., p. 100.
27 Schreiter, R. J. (1985) *Constructing Local Theologies*, p. 92. London: SCM.

2

Modern human identity

We saw in Chapter 1 that, throughout Judaeo-Christian history, shared human personal need has been the catalyst for pastoral response and theological creativity and, in so doing, have seen how people in need have been understood. We will now consider, briefly, how other religions and secular ideologies have identified the personal in different ways and how that has given rise to different understandings of how pastoral needs should be met.

We need a much greater knowledge of how different religions understand the personal and the pastoral. In what follows we will consider briefly its place in Islamic, Hindu and Buddhist thought along with reflections about the implications of religious pluralism for our understanding of the personal. Secular ideologies also have a profound impact on the way we understand the personal and this has been particularly true of our culture in the mid and late twentieth century. There are several of them and this is a reflection of the pluralistic nature of our times. Perhaps, and we can never be quite sure, this was not quite the case in the past when there was probably more general agreement about personal identity. We need to understand something of these ideologies and how they have affected human understanding and, in turn, care for humans, before we go on to consider how the Christian understanding of the personal and the pastoral fits into the modern world. The ones discussed in what follows have been chosen because they have all had a marked, if often diffuse, influence on the popular ways in which the personal is now understood. In conclusion, the Christian understanding of the personal will be outlined and advocated.

All pastoral care is interpersonal, as we have seen, and for this reason it is always possible to ask of any pastoral attitude or action: what view of the personal underlies this? The importance of understanding the personal in this way has recently received attention in moral philosophy and this is particularly relevant to pastoral studies. For example, in *After Virtue*, Alasdair MacIntyre argues that one reason for what he observes to be a contemporary crisis in morality is that it has lost its older classical and religious roots and embraced, often exclusively and uncritically, the legacy of the Enlightenment. By this, he means that under the influence of eighteenth-century rationalists, such as Jeremy Bentham and his successors, the essence of morality has been reduced, entirely and mistakenly, to a form of rational calculation. In Bentham's case this sought to quantify pleasure and pain and to maximize the former.[1] According to MacIntyre, this fails to take into account a vital dimension of what it means to be moral; the human. Correcting this requires, he argues, the study of three things: (i) untutored human nature, (ii) man-as-he-could-be-if-he-realized-his-telos, and, (iii) the moral precepts which enable him to pass from one state to the other.[2] The modern rationalist rejection of Aristotelian, Catholic and Protestant ethics under the influence of the Enlightenment, MacIntyre claims, has caused all notion of (ii) to be lost. As a consequence, he argues, moral thinking is in crisis because it has no vision of the true end of humankind. When this is redressed, he continues, it follows that moral values are something like expressions of human worth. That is, in a statement such as 'X' ought to do 'Y', 'Y' is an expression of the value of 'X'.[3]

In *After Virtue* MacIntyre draws heavily on Aristotle and on older Greek philosophy in this argument and stresses that 'man' is a functional noun. In this way he draws attention to the importance of understanding the end or purpose of human existence. Human beings on this view are *for* something. They do not exist without purpose. All this presupposes, of course, that humankind does have a true end. But what if, as has been observed, it does not? If this is the case, morality may well be something like the eighteenth-century rationalists, and others, have said it is. It may well be observed, therefore, that MacIntyre, in stressing his views in support of an older understanding of morality, has understated the probably equal importance of the modern alternatives. Whether we like it or not, because of the ubiquitous influence of the Enlightenment, we instinctively suppose to some degree or other that moral analyses have, at least, something to do with

evaluating the desirability or otherwise of the consequences of our contemplated actions. That, however, does not necessarily mean that MacIntyre's
point about the necessity of remembering the nature of humankind and its
purpose when we analyse morality is not a powerful one. Moreover, it is
highly unlikely that a single account of the nature of morality will ever be
discovered, it is far too mysterious for that. Perhaps, as has been suggested,
it is better to see morality as light is seen through a prism.[4] If so, then it is
unwise to exclude any elements from that prism. We will return to this
subject in the final chapter.

The relevance of this discussion of moral philosophy to pastoral theology
will now become clear. Pastoral actions, like moral ones, are also expressions of human worth. They may well also be considered as expressions of
other things, but they are at least this. The question, therefore, arises: how
do we choose an account of human worth? There are, of course, many
accounts to choose from be they religious or secular. The truth is that we
probably have such choices made for us, largely by the place, time and
accident of our birth. But that does not excuse us from considering the
implications of the question: what view of the personal do, or should, we
presuppose in our pastoral actions? It will help us to answer this question if
we consider some examples of such views which are important in our own
time in the sense that they influence, directly and indirectly, the way people
behave pastorally and ethically.

In a ground-breaking book on comparative religion first published in
1962, and still widely discussed, Wilfred Cantwell Smith argued for the
abolition of the noun 'religion' on the grounds that it means too many
diverse things.[5] Religions, he argues, only have names because we have
inadvertently and perhaps uncritically given them to them. His main reason,
however, for wanting to abolish the use of the term is because it calls our
attention to the wrong thing; to religions as self-contained competing
systems. This simple, but according to him mistaken, assumption in its turn
gives birth to the study of religions as discrete entities as well as to the study
of their comparative relationships. In place of the term 'religion', Cantwell
Smith wants us to use terms like 'piety' or 'religiousness' so that we look,
rather, for what is dynamic about the many faith traditions, how they
develop in their cumulative traditions and manifest themselves in the
personal and social lives of individuals.[6] This powerful observation has been
much taken up in subsequent discussions about religious pluralism, but it is
worth noticing for our purposes because of its pastoral implications. It calls
our attention to the fact that the most important thing about faith traditions

is how they enable their followers to lead and fulfil their lives. In his later *Towards a World Theology* he claims that 'the move ... is in our day through and beyond the several theologies of comparative religion or their counterparts that might be essayed towards something still more universal ...'.[7] He goes on to acknowledge that this something will hardly be a simple unifying account of religion, but he does claim that looking for it will give us as clear a picture as we are likely to find of what faith traditions, as he prefers to call them, are actually about.

One recent attempt to focus our attention in this way can be found in *The Oxford Dictionary of World Religions*. John Bowker, its editor, claims that what the major religions have all achieved is that they have made it possible for their followers to understand life as a 'project', 'religions make life as a project a little easier. They protect and transmit the means to attain the most important goals imaginable.'[8] These goals, he adds, include those which are proximate in that they deal with immediate matters and those which are ultimate.

Both Cantwell Smith and Bowker encourage us to find the essence of religion in studying what it does for its followers, rather in the way we studied Judaism and Christianity in Chapter 1. The more we do this the more likely we are, of course, to discover the profound similarities between religions and, even more importantly, to do so in ways which do not make the differences between them an *a priori* assumption. With these reflections in mind we will briefly consider how the three other major religions; Islam, Hinduism and Buddhism address pastoral well-being. Each of these religions exist in diverse forms and these will vary in the way they place their emphases on pastoral matters. What follows is, therefore, only a general outline.[9]

The pastoral in major non-Christian religions

Islam

Muslims believe that Allah has made it legislatively clear in the Qur'an what he requires of his followers. The Muslim life is, therefore, one of obedience to the will of Allah. It is lived out, first of all, in the strict observance of the institutions and rituals of their religion, some of which focus on Mecca and the concept of pilgrimage. Prayer is required five times a day and piety is derived from obedience to the will of Allah. Similarly to Christianity, this has produced a wide spectrum of religious piety ranging from the ascetic to the worldly in which eminent leaders have been revered, even after their deaths. The relationship between the various sorts of spiritual guides and their followers has been widely seen as the source of piety and personal well-being. Devotion to guides and to Allah is often indistinguishable and evidence of its quality is demonstrated through the observance of the minutiae of ritual requirement. This devotion fills the gaps in the practicalities of life which are left because the Qur'an does not legislate for everything in life the believer has to deal with. It explains, in no small measure, why Islamic leaders so often assume positions of seemingly awesome authority. Those of latter-day Iran and similarly conservative Islamic regimes stand in a long tradition in which the deference they receive is tempered with slavish obedience which, from the outside, seems to border on fear. From the inside, no doubt, all this is more than compensated for by the experience of spiritual assurance such devotion makes possible.

Morality in Islam is, then, interwoven with strict religious observance and a number of themes are recurrent. The requirements of justice permeate them all and this is linked directly to the avenging wrath of Allah. Little wonder that Islamic states demand of moral offenders severe reprisals for often minor offences and the death penalty for major ones. This seeming harshness is tempered by Allah's mercy and is the reason why severe sentences are frequently not carried out. The fact that this generally results in communities which are crime free when compared with many Western and more liberal ones is frequently observed. As a result, Westerners are invariably uneasy about the harshness of Islamic political regimes, but cannot always articulate precisely why. In all this there is no distinction, at least in theory, between the sacred and the secular since the secular is fully legislated for, either in the Qur'an or subsequent teaching. This is the reason why the sort of preoccupations with secular pastoral matters, which are so much a feature of Christian pastoral concerns, are not found in the same way in Islam. There simply is no sphere of life which is separate from the all-prevailing and legislatively clear will of Allah. The rule of the state is religious will. The way in which Christian pastoral concerns in the West now have to be exercised through secular legislation could not be more different though they do mirror, of course, more tolerant and liberal Islamic nations.

The similarities between strict Islamic societies and those where orthodox Judaism prevails are obvious. The social orders which result are, not surprisingly, conservative ones. They depend upon custom and convention and are least good at dealing with innovation and novelty. This is why they often find it so difficult to relate to Western societies where, for good or ill, the opposite is so often the case. It is at this point that frictions and differences emerge; for example, over the treatment of women. The Qur'an is more radical than Muslim practice often indicates. The Prophet is portrayed as showing respect for his wives and men and women are thought to be equal under Allah. The society out of which the Qur'an came, however, was quite otherwise. Women were seen as the property of their male consorts and female babies were buried alive with impunity and these tensions still survive in the socially static Muslim communities. Another marked difference concerns the freedom of literary expression, as the notorious fatwah (divine pronouncement) against Salman Rushdie continues to illustrate. Whilst all religions have the capacity to generate collective fanaticism, Islam is perhaps more prone to it than some, given the emphasis it places on the certainty of its knowledge of what Allah requires in every walk of life individually and socially. The historic clash between Islam and Christianity, today more manifest in the clash between Islam and Western culture, arises from the fact that both religions are missionary ones.

It should never be overlooked that Islam has produced one of the world's greatest civilizations and made incomparable contributions to its arts and sciences. Through these means alone its contribution to the betterment of the human lot has been immense and its achievement in these areas is a continuing one. It has also inculcated a markedly positive attitude to the present in the sense that its followers seek to observe the will of Allah, not because it will reap reward for them, but simply because for them it is the truth. There is none of the Christian restlessness for the Kingdom here. It is enough only that Allah's will be done. The spirituality of Islam and its pastoral sense are one and the same thing and they are, as we have seen, brought to bear through attention to the minutest of detail in the disciplines of the spiritual life.

Hinduism

The Hindu family of religious traditions are among the oldest in the world. They arose out of a synthesis of two of its great ancient civilizations; the Aryan and that of the Indus valley. This, alone, explains why Hinduism is as diverse in its forms as it is rich in content. It is more helpful to think of this tradition less as *a* religion than as a diverse family of related traditions. Little wonder that it is a difficult religious tradition to generalize about. What briefly follows is an attempt to sketch in outline some of its recurrent pastoral features.

Striving for self-realization is a distinctive theme in Hindu spirituality. It focuses on the desire to conform the individual true self (Atman) to the Cosmic self (Brahman). This striving requires a dedicated searching after the true nature of reality which is the source of saving knowledge. There are many ways in which this striving is carried out in the different Hindu traditions. Some emphasize the importance of the use of reason, in others the distinction between matter and the soul is the key to enlightenment and in others the emphasis is on worship and ritual. In these and other ways the Hindu traditions span the whole spectrum of religious engagements and endeavours. The striving for enlightenment is a markedly human endeavour which presupposes that human resources can lead the soul to Brahman. The religious life, so understood, is one which is made up of those practices which the individual believes will lead to enlightenment and, in turn, to the end of rebirth. All manner of countless lesser deities are called upon in local manifestations of Hinduism to assist with this ongoing process of enlightenment. These lesser and noticeably worldly deities do not compete with Brahman, they are all but earthly manifestations of what is eternal and alone of real worth – Brahman. The devotion these lesser deities require, however, is absolute. All this is far from the fears of idolatry found in the Judaeo-Christian religious traditions. As in all religious traditions, there is widespread veneration for and devotion to teachers of enlightenment in Hinduism. They are seen as the gurus who live and work in the service of the great guru the Lord Krishna.

In contrast to the diversity of Hindu spirituality, three great moral / spiritual requirements are laid upon all Hindus. They are the so-called three Ds: Damyata which requires self restraint and control, Datta which requires giving, and Dayadhavam which requires compassion. Meeting these requirements is impossible unless the soul is purified and sin restrained. Again, in contrast with Christianity, sin is thought of not as something which afflicts the individual by dint of inner nature, but as something which afflicts from without and which, by appropriate means can be kept at bay. Carnal desire, wrath and greed are its most common manifestations and their presence in human life, in even mild forms, prohibit the end of the soul's rebirth. This radical and demanding approach to spirituality explains why the path to enlightenment is so steep and why the endeavour to achieve it must be unceasing.

The emphasis on individual enlightenment in Hinduism, as contrasted with group enlightenment and self-interest, has had the effect of making it a socially conservative way of life in the sense that it accepts the givenness of social institutions in general. This fact goes a long way to throw light on why the non-violent struggles of Gandhi against British rule in India in pursuit of independence were not typical of the widespread Hindu resignation to whatever is socially given, though Gandhi was rightly seen by some to be the heir to older nineteenth-century Hindu reform movements. His assassination in 1948 by more strict Hindus, was motivated in part by the belief that, by his actions, he was violating the sacred deities and incurring their wrath.

In Hindu life generally, the divine presence is something which is thought of as all-pervading. Herein lies what is, perhaps, seen from the outside, its central paradox from a pastoral point of view. Hinduism is at one and the same time world-renouncing and world-accepting. This paradox is redeemed, however, by the sort of inter-personal disposition required by the three Ds we have mentioned above. The typical Hindu, if there ever is such a person, is therefore someone who is extremely tolerant of her or his social circumstances and yet, also, gracious towards others in the context of an all-pervading religious life. That there are few shared tangible manifestations of the Hindu spiritual virtues no doubt arises from the fact that it is a religious life of millions of people lived out in a wide diversity of social, political and economic circumstances. Its powerful sense of the past and veneration of the antiquity of its central institutions is probably another reason why there is less focus on specific and more recognizably pastoral issues such as those found in the Western religious traditions. The lack of central orthodoxies and the credal uniformity they facilitate is, again, another stark contrast with the Western religions and a further clue as to why it is that the pastoral dispositions of the two different sorts of approach to the religious life are equally impossible to compare directly. Both, however, are equally important manifestations of the human religious experience and both, in their own way, throw light on what it means to be fully human in the divine presence, however differently that is understood.

Buddhism

Buddhism, like Hinduism, came from India where it is now a minority religion, and has spread throughout the Eastern countries in each of which it has assumed distinctive characteristics. It dates from the time of the Buddha (500 BCE) and its central message is beautifully simple; all life suffers in a wide sense, which includes frustrations and inadequacies, and needs to be healed. This was the essential teaching expressed in the 'Dharma', and the means whereby it is achieved is through its manifestation in community, the 'Samgha'. In spite of the great variety of forms Buddhism has taken, this simple message remains constant in all of them. It has produced a religious tradition which focuses on the practicalities of morality and everyday life rather than on gods and metaphysical entities. Like Hinduism, however, Buddhism does embrace the spiritual aid of innumerable lesser deities. The spiritual preoccupations, however, are very much with the here and now. They are not codified in anything that the West would easily recognize as an ethical system as such. The emphasis, rather, is on the practicalities of overcoming suffering amid the practicalities of life. The virtues of truthfulness (supremely), tolerance and benevolence are prominent in all Buddhist teaching, as are repeated warnings against covetousness. Again, in contrast with Western religions there is less emphasis on justice as such, though issues of justice are embraced in the Buddhist striving for a 'right livelihood' and the outworking of its social implications. However, traditionally at least, Buddhism is probably the least socially active and engaged of all the major religious traditions.

It is often observed, for example, that wars have never been fought in the name of the Buddha. This, of course, can be taken in two ways. It can be seen as being highly commendable, when contrasted with the extent to which most of the other religions have been so involved and not always to their credit, or it can be seen as evidence of the unacceptable degree to which Buddhism eschews this world in favour of what might be seen as self-indulgent spiritual absorption. At its most extreme, this resulted in the Bhikku life of (male) celibacy and spiritual absorption. Around each group of these there are many lay orders. These are deemed to achieve an enlightenment which is sufficient for salvation. Whether or not they do this depends on the law of Karma; a seeking after knowledge which leads to the absorption of causation and action amid the practicalities of everyday life. This is the area of the spiritual life in which it is decided whether or not reincarnation and rebirth can be achieved. Buddhism shares with other Asian religions, at this point, the belief that all actions have consequences for good or evil and that these reverberate for eternity. Unlike the other similar religions, however, Buddhism does not believe that there is a 'self' which can be reborn. Rebirth, rather, will be into a suffering-free stream of consciousness in which there is an accumulation of good rather than, simply, reward for individuals.

The teaching of the Buddha is condensed into the so-called Four Noble Truths. These are: (a) recognition of the all pervasive nature of suffering, (b) an understanding of what causes the suffering, (c) a realization that suffering can be ceased and, (d) the means whereby (c) is achieved by following the Eightfold Path to enlightenment.

In contrast to an image many have of Buddhism as an asocial religion, some modern Buddhist scholars are addressing more worldly concerns, such as Aids, in ways which enable them to make contributions to wider debates about social issues. As South East Asia becomes increasingly industrialized and economically more complex, the challenge of wider ethical concerns arising from these factors will provide a real test for Buddhist spirituality. It will either have to embrace them by showing how they can be coped with in the light of ancient Buddhist teaching, or it will become an increasingly marginalized religious way of life for the majority who will inevitably be caught up in these processes. The same can, of course, be observed about Hinduism, particularly in a country like India which is already among the most industrialized in the world. Either both of these great religious traditions will develop in ways which meet these changing circumstances, or they will be ignored, or they will exist only to provide syncretistic refuge from the increasing demands of secularism.

If we were but able to compare pieties in the way Cantwell Smith has encouraged us to do, rather than allowing the simplicity of that to be frustrated by notions of religious differences, the quality of the pastoral dialogue between Christianity and the other major faith traditions would be greatly improved and all would benefit. The degree to which old suspicions cast shadows over us when we attempt this, is frightening. At the very least, those who seek pastoral insight into the human condition from religious points of view should try to befriend each other, mutually understand their faith traditions and, above all, share common concern for the welfare of all human beings.

Just as the Christian constructing of pastoral theology has to come to terms with that in other religions, so it has also to come to terms with the focus of pastoral concerns in secular philosophies and movements. Only when it does this can it begin to understand its wider place in the worldwide quest for human well-being.

In what follows, therefore, we will: (a) consider four twentieth-century approaches to the personal; (b) briefly show something of the pastoral attitudes which have been derived from them; and (c) bring some critical reflections to bear on them. We will then outline the Christian approach to the personal and show how that offers a more intellectually and pastorally acceptable basis for understanding what happens when people care for each other than do the alternative views. However, in being critical of these alternative views of the personal, we will not deny that they contain certain fundamental insights which have to be remembered. But as complete accounts of the personal these four approaches represent, in different ways, only partial insights, when judged as an account of the whole. These four approaches are: the evolutionary / biological; the Marxist / sociological; the existentialist; and the positivist. These have appeared in many guises as well as in unlikely coalition with each other, but for clarity and convenience we will examine them separately.

Views of the personal

Evolutionary

This view had its origin in the nineteenth century and a version of it has been made widely popular in books such as those by Desmond Morris, namely *The Naked Ape* and *The Human Zoo*.[10] The writings of Alex Comfort are other more recent examples of this view.[11] It is derived from the Darwinian claim that humans are biologically the most evolved of all creatures and that evolution has been due to random mutation and natural selection, working in accord with chance environmental changes. In *The Origin of Species* (1859) Darwin brought a mass of inductive evidence to bear on a long-held hypothesis and, in so doing, believed that he had demonstrated two facts about humankind: (a) that it had not been separately created, and (b) that humankind's appearance as distinct creatures could be explained, as could the differences between all living creatures, on the basis of natural selection. Whilst this theory left room for metaphysical speculation about the divine origin of humankind, it did not strictly require it. In a later work, *The Descent of Man*, Darwin further argued that humankind's moral capacities also originated from its animal descent. As proof of this he cited the fact that initial social impulses which give rise to conscience are to be observed among young animals. From this Darwin concluded that humankind's moral capacity does not distinguish it at all from animals, and that this capacity, just like any other, could be transmitted by heredity. He did have some doubts about this last claim, and it is still often the subject of debate.

Twenty years later Herbert Spencer took these ideas a stage further, in *The Data of Ethics*, and argued that humankind's conduct evolved just as everything else about it did. Spencer describes this evolution as that displayed by the highest type of being when forced, by increase of numbers, to live in close proximity. All moral ideas, Spencer held, are related to this general principle. In other words, morality is but an aspect of the general observation that only the fittest survive; an expression of ruthless self-interest. Although doubts were expressed about this view in the late nineteenth century, such as those in T. H. Huxley's Romanes Lectures of 1883 (where it was observed that ethics suggests that the strong should care for the weak and that this seemed to contradict natural selection, where the strong look after themselves), the general view, that humankind is an evolved and evolving species, carried the day. It was part of and, indeed, also largely responsible for a much more widespread liberal optimism about the inevitability of social as well as natural progress.

For reasons explained earlier, that optimism came to an abrupt end, but the view that humankind is to be understood solely with reference to its biological origin has survived. In *The Naked Ape*, Desmond Morris bluntly states: 'There are one hundred and ninety-three living species of monkeys and apes. One hundred and ninety-two of them are covered with hair. The exception is a naked ape, self-named Homo sapiens.'[12] To Morris, a zoologist, the naked ape-human is first and foremost an animal. For all humankind's sophistication and erudition the fact remains. When discussing sexual relations, for example, Morris considers that humankind owes all its basic sexual qualities to its fruit-picking forest-ape ancestors. In *The Human Zoo* Morris adds that in the healthy adult human male and female there is a basic physiological requirement for repeated sexual consummation.

Here, then, is a clear anthropology, a confident attempt to explain the essential nature of humankind. If we are to accept it as an adequate basis for pastoral theology certain things will follow, as they have done in the view of some for sexual ethics. This would encourage people to do whatever they felt was in accord with their basic instinctive desires, on the grounds that these have to be satisfied if they are to flourish. Certain aspects of the Encounter Group movement can be understood in this light. In it people are often encouraged to cast away inhibitions and to give expression to their innermost desires. In this way they can be liberated from social and other inhibitions which demand that they behave in ways which are alien to their natures as the highest primates. Some types of sexual therapy counselling can also be seen to have been influenced by such views. They often attempt to demystify sex by making it more matter-of-fact, thereby emphasizing its role as a normal and vital human activity.

Is this view of human nature acceptable? Is it true that in all our dealings with people we must presuppose that we and they are naked apes? There is one undoubted attraction to this view. It stresses that human well-being is an integral part of the well-being of the rest of creation. Humans are seen as standing within a 'life chain' which must not be broken if they are to survive and flourish. The view that humans are 'naked apes' therefore encourages, and even demands, a degree of ecological seriousness which has only very recently begun to be at all widely accepted. There is much to commend this, since it can hardly be overstressed that, if humans are to flourish, then they must pay urgent attention to the management of their environment. This insight perhaps represents the highest achievement of the evolutionary view of human nature and it is one which must not be lost sight of, in spite of the fact that much of the thinking which lies behind it has long since been open to question and criticism. Certainly, up to the outbreak of the First World War, the view was coupled with the optimistic belief that life was getting inevitably better, on the grounds that personal and social values evolved just as biological organisms do. Views about the inevitability of social progress were closely linked in this way to views about biological progress and, indeed, were often inseparable from them. Even the prospect of war in 1914 did not immediately threaten this optimism about the inevitability of progress. Many volunteered for military service in the belief that the war would hasten the dawn of a better tomorrow. The truth, of course, was quite the reverse. The scale of the suffering caused, along with a growing confusion about its purpose, soon showed that such progress was far from inevitable. Although the nineteenth-century theory of biological evolution has largely survived intact, the views of morality and human identity which were once confidently associated with it are now less commonly found.

Marxism

The influence of Marxism on the modern world is immense, notwithstanding its recent eclipse as a philosophy which is capable of sustaining monolithic political and economic structures, as throughout the world communist-style command economies are giving way to market ones in what are often destabilizing circumstances. The fact remains, however, that many of the world's developing nations use versions of Marxism to structure their emergent nationalisms although they are now commonly tempered with versions of free market economics. For these reasons Marxism will continue to have an immense influence on the understanding of the personal and its well-being especially in its social dimensions.

Marx was basically concerned with understanding human freedom, as well as with discovering how to attain that freedom through human co-operation. This freedom, he argued, could only be achieved if humankind itself removed the obstacles which stood in its way. And these, Marx argued, were entirely of human making. In making this point, Marx distinguished, as Descartes had done before him, between human experience and the external world; distinguished, that is, between consciousness-of-the-world and the-world-itself. From this he constructed a vision of humans as free agents who, above everything, are capable of changing the world simply because they are distinct from it. In a vein that was later to be developed by Nietzsche, Marx repeatedly emphasized that human freedom can only be acquired through revolution. The two main obstacles which stood in the way of human freedom he identified as the State and money. Both were institutionalized expressions of the way in which humans are robbed of their freedom, their worst examples being found in feudalism and capitalism respectively. The more servile humans are, as in the former, and the more productive they are, as in the latter, the greater their alienation becomes, both from the object of their servility and from the products of their labour. This alienation threatens them in basic ways. The goods they produce pass into private ownership and people then have to compete with each other for that ownership, thereby producing class struggles as sectional interests compete to gain advantage over each other. Because the earth's natural and finite resources are used to sustain all this, those who take part in the struggle also become alienated from their environment. Thus people become the victims of factors which *appear* to be external to them, rendering them seemingly helpless as the result of an illusion. Marx's point here was to stress that what humans had made they could change. The changes which are invariably necessary, however, are so great that they can only be called revolutionary ones.

From this basic understanding of the nature of human freedom and the causes of its impediments, Marx and those who followed him developed their view of human nature. It is a view which at its best holds out the possibility of help to the helpless and of nobility to the downtrodden. In many of its more recent versions it has been seen by many Christians, for example, as standing for what they stand for in a common hope for justice with fairness. There are, consequently, many coalitions of Marxism and Christianity to be found throughout the world, notably in Latin America and parts of Asia. More generally, many contemporary examples of thinking about the personal in the West are, directly and indirectly, derived from Marxism. Sociology and economics are just two branches of knowledge which are often indebted to it. Tracing the influence of Marxism on the twentieth-century understanding of the personal would, however, be an immense task. All we can do here is to note, as we have done, some of its main features.

In Christian pastoral theology, there has often been a tendency to divorce pastoral care from social and political concerns. To understand the classic expression of Christian pastoral care, the washing of feet, by thinking only of the deed itself without also thinking of the reasons why feet require washing, is to understand pastoral care in a way which divorces it from the world around it. A contemporary example of this can be found in the charitable work which was done by Mother Teresa and continued by many of those who are inspired by her example. Whilst all she did and stood for was courageous in the extreme and imbued with spirituality, it was, in India at least, strictly apolitical. The victims of society were cared for as they were found without much apparent parallel care for and concern about changing the unacceptable social and economic structures which were responsible for their condition in the first place. Whilst the intrinsic value of Mother Teresa's work is not diminished by this observation, it should encourage those who admire it to recognize the fact that it raises certain profound and uneasy questions about the limited way in which it was carried out by her and still is by many of her followers. Care for the afflicted must, if it is to be complete, give rise to equal care for and concern to remove the political causes of their afflictions.

Classical Marxism now has for many a somewhat tarnished image especially in view of the historically recent collapse of so many of the political systems for which it was for so long *de rigeur*. Some Neo-Marxists have recognized that many societies and economies which have developed under Marxist guidance have had serious drawbacks but have, nevertheless, retained a respect for what remains profound about what Marx said about human nature. This has resulted in a willingness to discuss with others questions of human values and human culpability and this, in turn, has created a framework for dialogue between Marxists and others, such as some Christians, who believe that the Kingdom of God should have some relevance to this world and its socio-political institutions. The liberation theologies are as we have seen, in their different ways, often the outcome of such collaboration.

Existentialism

'Existentialism' is often loosely used to describe a wide variety of views about human nature. The slogan 'existence precedes essence' is, however, usually taken as a convenient way of describing what binds those views together. This stresses that the basis of all knowledge is self-knowledge and shows also that humans, if they but realize it, have an endless capacity for self-analysis and improvement, providing they do not shun or try to deny the extent of their own powers. A brief description of some of the views of J-P. Sartre will illustrate these themes. In his major systematic work, *Being and Nothingness*, Sartre stresses that self-knowledge begins with an awareness of the distinction between the self and the external world.[13] Interestingly, for all the difference between existentialism and Marxism, they thus begin from remarkably identical starting-points and thereby show their common indebtedness to Descartes who famously distinguished between the knowledge we have of our own existence and the distinction which exists between that and the knowledge we have of the external world. According to Sartre, being is isolated and does not enter into any connection with non-being. This being, or consciousness, is what enables individuals to negate their knowledge of things which have no consciousness and it is what distinguishes the conscious individual from the external world. For Sartre, this consciousness is the source of individual freedom. Most beings find the loneliness of their own freedom too much to bear, with the result that they do all they can to pretend that they are like the things in the world around them which have no freedom. They do this by exercising what Sartre calls 'bad faith', which is the pretence that they are not free. Among the many literary illustrations which Sartre gave of this, that of the waiter in a café is the most quoted. A waiter denies his own individuality by playing the *role* of a waiter, in a way which does not allow his own feelings to have any part. Pretence, slavishness and convention therefore prevail, and the waiter's own identity is lost, even from his own sight.

The influence which existentialism continues to have on thinking about the personal cannot be overestimated. It has inspired, among other things, a whole popular culture which has worshipped the principle of 'doing one's own thing', sometimes to the point of glorifying selfishness. At a more profound level, however, it also provided no small part of the rationale

behind the European reconstruction of the notion of individual responsibility in the aftermath of Nazism and other mass movements where
individualism was subsumed and denied.

An example of the effect of existentialism on the study of pastoral care
can be found in the writings of Carl Rogers. One of Rogers' fundamental
principles is that nothing is to be done which compromises another's
freedom. Accordingly, counselling must be non-directive, value judgements
are to be avoided, and others are not to be given ethical advice on the
grounds that giving it would compromise their individuality and freedom to
act in their own interest. We will discuss some of the implications of this
view in Chapter 4. Sartre himself became notorious for refusing to give a
young man ethical advice when he asked for it at the end of a lecture. More
widely, the so-called 'new morality' owed much to this view of freedom, with
the result that as much attention came to be paid to *how* things were done as
had traditionally been given to *what* things were done. Lord Shawcross
tartly dismissed this view of morality as 'the old immorality condoned', and
so it seemed to those who failed to understand many of the presuppositions
which lay behind it; presuppositions which came largely from existentialist
writers. Existentialism provides a graphic and compelling vision of what it
means for individuals to take themselves seriously, perhaps at times too
seriously.

Again, however, whenever this view of human nature is taken as anything
other than a partial insight, distortion occurs. Its main weakness is that it
provides no way in which humans are understood as social beings; indeed, it
even argues that to understand them as such is to misunderstand their
nature. There is no clear path from an existentialist understanding of the
personal to an understanding of the individual's place in society. In stressing
the importance of individuality, it lost sight of the related importance of
community. As we have briefly seen, the historical context of modern
existentialism goes some way to explaining why this came about. Sartre
himself became increasingly aware of these difficulties and, as a result,
joined the Communist party. Disillusionment with it set in, however, after
the Russians invaded Czechoslovakia as well as Hungary, and he resigned
from the party in protest. To the end of his life, however, Sartre retained a
respect for communism, especially Italian communism.

The influence of existentialism on the understanding of the personal
remains and, providing it is understood in the context of other understandings with which it often has to be reconciled even with some difficulty,
that influence will be a wholly beneficial one. The main reason for this is the

obvious fact that it stands as a compelling corrective to all forms of collectivism which engulf the individual and deny freedom. It also helps to engender a sense of what it means to own responsibility for our actions.

Positivism

Positivism is the name for yet another twentieth-century philosophy and more general outlook which has had immense implications for the understanding of the personal. More recently, it has been known as 'logical positivism', which A. J. Ayer, its leading English exponent, described as being just like the older positivism of the nineteenth century, but combined with the rigours of the newer, twentieth-century, logic. Following earlier empiricist philosophers, Ayer held, in *Language, Truth and Logic* (1936), that the self was nothing but a 'logical construction out of the sense-experiences which constitute the actual and possible sense-history of a self'.[14] It follows from this that it is misleading to think of the self as a substance. From the fact, therefore, that humans are continually conscious of themselves nothing can be postulated about the existence of that, beyond what is contained in the conscious awareness. However, in an attempt to avoid some of the more obvious nihilistic consequences of this view, Ayer argued that personal identity could be re-established on the basis of a phenomenalist understanding of what it was that bound successive sense perceptions together. He says little about this, however, which distances him at all from nihilistic philosophers, such as David Hume, with whom he was in essential agreement on this topic. The background of Ayer's thinking about the self is to be found in what he said about meaning, which was central to his philosophy, namely, that the only statements which could be considered meaningful *at all* were those which were meaningful according to the 'verification principle', according to which, any statement which was neither tautologous nor empirically verifiable in sense experience was to be considered meaningless.[15]

A number of views about the personal were derived, directly and indirectly, from logical positivism and from the older positivism which preceded it. The so-called 'behavioural sciences' are particularly indebted to it. What these have in common is the presupposition that the only things which can be said about humans at all meaningfully are those things which are capable of scientific observation and measurement. For this reason, much attention was paid by the behaviourists to the interaction between humans and their environment. For example, the radical behaviourist, B. F. Skinner, goes so far as to deny any possibility of understanding human behaviour by analysing its inner causes.[16] He is, therefore, opposed both to the analytical psychology of Freud and Jung and the existential psychology of Rollo May and others. What Skinner and other behaviourists propose is the radical theory that human behaviour is *solely* determined by external conditioning.

The behavioural therapies have been developed in acceptance of and response to this view. They, therefore, attempt to 'target' behavioural disorders and deal with their external causes. This approach, they claim, marks an important advance on the interminable and unverifiable speculations of analytic and existential psychologies. At their most extreme, some behaviourists even claimed that total human flourishing could only be achieved by environmental manipulation. Some architects and planners, for example, worked on the assumption that what they did could alone change humans for the better. The grandiose scale of many of their schemes, along with their frequent and manifest impracticability, may now be seen as standing for a fundamentally mistaken view of the nature of the relationship between humans and their environment. Here again is a view of human nature which contains partial insights. It shows, at the very least, that the relationship between humans and their environment is an important one which cannot be ignored. What it has, however, singularly failed to show is that the whole truth about human nature and its flourishing can be so understood. Behaviourism does not justify us in supposing, without question, that humans can be cared-for simply by manipulating the environment in which they live, or in thinking that we can confine our exclusive attention to whatever else about them might be susceptible to scientific observation, measurement and analysis.

Christianity

So far in this chapter we have, briefly, considered the place of the pastoral in the principal Eastern religious traditions and seen how four twentieth-century views of the personal have led to pastoral implications. In addition, we have indicated some of the shortcomings of these views whilst acknowledging, generally, that they all say something important about human nature. There is clearly a need, and a practical one at that, for a wider view of human nature which is capable of recognizing the value of such insights, as and when it may be appropriate to do so, but which is also capable of providing them with a context within which they can be accepted or criticized as necessary.

It will now be argued that the mainstream Christian understanding of human nature does provides such a framework. It is one which contains its own distinctive elements and yet is, at the same time, able to take into consideration important discoveries contained in other religious and secular insights, such as those we have been discussing. Whether or not what will now be explored will be thought at all adequate, will depend largely on how one goes about assessing such adequacy. In the end, it is probably not possible to do anything more for the beliefs by which we live than to claim that they fit the facts as we see them, and that they, therefore, provide a more adequate account of such facts than we can hope to obtain from elsewhere.

This mainstream Christian understanding of human nature recognizes first and foremost that it is a mystery. In claiming that humans are created in the image of God, Christianity roots the mystery about them in the mystery of God. Just as everything cannot be known about an infinite God by finite humans, so also humans will never know all there is to know about themselves simply because their nature participates in the infinity of the divine nature. Christian teaching about immortality, for example, can be understood in this way, since it follows from this belief that humans are to be understood as living a life which goes beyond the present one because their being participates in the immortality of the divine being. Another aspect of the Christian understanding of human nature follows from this; namely, that this life is lived constantly under the judgement of a righteous God. This is what gives humans an awareness of their basic sinfulness and inadequacy. Furthermore, Christians claim that they know how this sinfulness can be overcome – by the grace and forgiveness of God. All this, of course, is to claim a great deal about human nature. Much of it will be uncongenial to those who hold alternative views, such as those we have been examining. But there is nothing in those views which rules such a Christian view out, particularly if it is able to embrace what is thought to be good about them in the ways we have seen. The Christian view, in fact, provides a more profound understanding of the human relation to the historical process, to the natural order, to individual experience, and to the environment than can be obtained by taking any of those secular views in isolation. Its relationship to other religions is, as we have seen, more complex and best understood alongside them as a way of handling life's practicalities.

Once it is recognized that what Christians have to say about the personal has practical applications, then it is possible to put aside, initially at least, the more speculative questions about its truth or falsity. Christians care for others, not just because they believe that they are alienated from themselves and nature, not just because they are the most evolved of all living species, not just because as individuals they are sacrosanct, nor because they are only creatures of their environment; but because they believe that they are created in the image of God. The profundity and the adequacy or otherwise of believing this will be discussed in the following chapters, but first we need to consider a fundamental objection to taking such a view.

It has often been supposed that pastoral care and counselling can take place without reference to any such views as those we have been discussing. Supposed, that is, that there is care and counselling and that this is an end to the matter. Such a view is, however, an extremely dangerous one. All care takes place within a moral and ultimately within a religious context, taking 'religious' in that sense to mean, as we have seen, views of life with some ultimate reference. It is simply not possible to exercise care for other human beings without presupposing and enacting certain values which relate closely to what we think about their identity. If practitioners of pastoral care fail to examine their presuppositions and choose to continue as though they do not exist, then they are placing themselves uncritically at the mercy of any prevailing and fashionable views. It is incumbent on those who are concerned with the understanding and exercise of pastoral care, in all its diversity, to examine the main presuppositions which inform their work, and, most importantly, those presuppositions they have about the nature of the personal itself. When this is done, we have seen that the Christian account of the personal demands just as much attention as any other. It follows from this conclusion that Christian pastoral care is distinguishable in part from other types of pastoral care because of the view of the personal which it presupposes. Like other views of pastoral care it has its own presuppositions about the personal without which, like them, it would be incoherent.

Whilst we have considered something of the many ways in which Christian pastoral care can avail itself of some of the insights of other approaches, there remains an important sense in which it is, arguably, distinct from them. Because Christianity is a revealed religion, then to be in this sense Christian, Christian pastoral care must embody what is revealed. It must, that is, be a proclaiming activity. It must embody the essential *kerygma* of the Christian gospel, which is a proclamation of redemption and salvation. For the most part, it will achieve this without overtly preaching in the traditional manner. But what it can never forget is that Christian pastoral care is but an aspect of the wider ministry of the word and sacraments which is of the essence of Christianity. We will consider the biblical and other origins of this in the next chapter. As a preliminary to that we will first consider some of the implications which arise when Christianity meets, as it inescapably does, other religions and their pastoral aspirations.

People might have an evangelistic motivation behind their pastoral care because they believe, quite properly, that their faith has something healing to offer the person, as is shown in the Gospels wherever Jesus implies that healing is linked to faith. Even this is pastorally problematic, however, and never more so than when the devout suffer. More crudely, Christian pastoral care can sometimes be little more than covert evangelism and not always covert at that. Some Christians will, moreover, suppose that pastoral theology is only to be engaged in for this purpose. To this it must be objected that personal need should be met pastorally for its own sake and not in the pursuit of some ulterior motives such as evangelism and conversion. The view individuals take at this point will depend on what they implicitly think about the status of Christianity in relation to other religions and ideologies. The view that pastoral theology and care is but an adjunct of Christian evangelism can follow naturally from a belief in the superiority of Christianity over other religions. If Christianity is thought to be the one true faith, then it is quite proper to want to enable people to enter it. Killing people to save their souls is an extreme example of this which is sadly not unknown in Christian history. Although most Christians would now recoil from such an interpretation of their faith, they, nevertheless, for the most part, cling to a view of the superiority of their religion over others and that it must in all things and in the end prevail over them. But is it socially, politically and pastorally realistic to suppose that Christianity will, or should, ever prevail in this way as the one true religion? Much hangs on the answer to this question since it affects every aspect of Christian theology, the pastoral included.

It is an incontrovertible fact that the numerical and territorial extent of the world's major religions – Christianity, Judaism, Islam, Hinduism and Buddhism – remains remarkably stable. People do, of course, convert from one to the other, but only in numbers which are insignificant. Growth in the overall number of Christians is now significantly limited by their widespread practice of birth control. By contrast, however, the number of Hindus is growing. It is no longer, therefore, realistic to suppose that Christianity, any more than any other religion, can inexorably be on track to achieving world domination. The same is, of course, true of secular ideologies, many of the proponents of which either have or are beginning to recognize this. With the world like it is, for better or worse, it is now imperative that peoples of different religions and secular ideologies learn to live with each other in peaceful coexistence. This is made necessary by the need to eliminate or at least control poverty and disease as well as contain and perhaps eliminate the threat of nuclear war and the annihilation which it would bring. In such a world, religious or secular ideologies which behave as though they have a right to world domination are unacceptably dangerous and serve only to prevent peaceful coexistence on a world-wide scale.

Some Christians who are aware of these issues respond by adopting what may be described as an 'inclusivist' as opposed to an 'exclusivist' attitude to other religions and ideologies.[17] In so doing they, often subtly, maintain a belief in the superiority of their own religion, but acknowledge that God works, although less perfectly, through other religions and ideologies. They further claim that, in so doing, God can bring about the salvation of members of other religions. Such a view is a marked improvement on the exclusivism criticized above and, properly exercised, it goes far to ameliorate the dangerous potential of the exclusivist position. But 'inclusivism' still embraces the fundamental precept of exclusivism; namely, that Christianity is in some sense superior to other religions. This is, to say the least, patronizing towards other religions and is so in the extreme when it allows only for the incomplete or less than perfect salvation of their adherents. This alone would be sufficient for the 'inclusivists' to behave in some ways like the 'exclusivists' whenever they are given the opportunity to do so. To return again to the work of W. Cantwell Smith, he calls for a religious 'pluralism' in which all the world's great religions are invited to recognize that they are but partial forms of access to the one true God.[18] In other words, all religions should be seen as being commonly theocentric, regardless of the nature of their particular belief in God. This latter qualification allows the ostensibly non-theistic religions such as Buddhism to be included in the definition. According to Cantwell Smith, what all the religions have in common is the faith they embrace in a cumulative tradition.

Again, the relevance of these remarks to pastoral theology will be obvious. Just as we have extended its study to include consideration of secular ideologies, we have also seen that it is necessary to examine its relationship to pastoral theologies of other religions. There is a need for a major comparative study in this area. This is, of course, a mammoth task and there has been space here to do no more than indicate its necessity in this way. This recognition, however, will alone do much to ensure that Christian pastoral theology is not used as an excuse for the exercise of a but thinly disguised group self-interest. Moreover, an approach such as that advocated by Cantwell Smith, opens the possibility of enabling Christians to bring to their pastoral theology and care an integrity which will be recognized as having a radically unselfish concern for the well-being of others regardless of their creed or secular ideology. All this is not to suppose that all religions and secular ideologies are in all respects pastorally equal. They are obviously not, which is why they always have much to learn from each other. As a result, they must be continually developed by self-critical reflection and dialogue. At its best, this has always been the case in Christian pastoral theology. For example, in the nineteenth century people came to realize that their centuries old acceptance of slavery as a social institution had been mistaken. Similarly, in the twentieth century, Christian pastoral thought is only now realizing that its, again centuries old, acceptance of the subordination of women is equally unacceptable.

An important point needs to be made in conclusion of this chapter and will be raised subsequently. What we have been calling theologies and anthropologies, religious and secular, seldom exist in pure form. And this is as true of Christianity as of any other religion or ideology. There may well be individuals who exemplify a religion or an ideology in a pure form to an intense degree, but when they do and are found in any numbers they often represent some fanaticism or other. That is not to say, of course, that there are not ardent and responsible exponents and defenders of discrete religions; there clearly are and they are important not the least as exemplars or possibly saints. It is but to suggest that, with the world as it now is, there needs to be an overlap in the pastoral vision between different religions and ideologies. Perhaps this has always been the case in some degree, but the need for such an overlap is now imperative. As observed earlier, the religion or ideology that we either profess or are influenced by is hardly ever something of our entirely free choice. To be rigorously eclectic we would have to begin from some value-free starting-point in order to select from other value systems whatever suited the purpose we were contemplating. Such value-free starting-points do not exist, although they have been attempted in pseudo-religions such as Theosophy. Indeed, what we call 'the secular' is not a value-free starting-point, as it is often thought to be. 'Secularity' is a heavily value-laden notion. As such, it is not available for use as a platform for criticism of other views which are more overtly and accountably value laden. It, therefore, follows that any approach to pastoral care from a secular standpoint is very much (in method) the same as approaching it from any other, including a religious one. This will be discussed in more detail in Chapter 4.

In this chapter we have briefly examined the distinctive nature of the Christian view of the personal. We have seen that it is able to embrace many of the insights found in alternative religious and secular accounts. It shares with other religions a concern to locate personal well-being amid the practicalities of life with reference to what is ultimate and of true worth. With the secular ideologies; it shares with the evolutionist the stress on the importance of physical needs; it shares with the Marxist the importance of recognizing collective human agency; it shares with the existentialist the stress on autonomy and individuality; and it shares with the positivist recognition of the role that the environment plays in shaping human destiny. However, it goes beyond these accounts in three ways. It stresses in its own way the mystery of personality, the fallenness of human nature, and the need for grace. Finally, we noted the need for a Christian anthropology to be pluralistic rather than imperialistic in relation to other faith traditions. It is in this spirit that we now turn to look more closely at the resources of the Christian tradition, to consider what we mean by understanding pastoral care from the point of view of Christian theology. Only when this is done will it be possible elsewhere to discuss the relationship of the Christian approach to that of others.

Notes

1   MacIntyre, A. (1981) *After Virtue*, p. 52. London: Duckworth.
2   Ibid.
3   For a critical discussion of this claim, see Hudson, W. D. (1983) *Modern Moral Philosophy* (second edition), pp. 367–71. London: Macmillan.
4   See Emmet, D. M. (1979) *The Moral Prism*, London: Macmillan.
5   Cantwell Smith, Wilfred (1962) *The Meaning and End of Religion*, p. 194. New York: Macmillan.
6   Ibid.
7   Cantwell Smith, Wilfred (1981) *Towards a World Theology*, p. 181. London: Macmillan.
8   Bowker, John, ed. (1997) *The Oxford Dictionary of World Religions*, p. xx. Oxford: Oxford University Press.
9   Two excellent guides for study in this area are Harris, I., Mews, S., Morris, P. and Shepard, J., eds (1994), *Longman Guide to Living Religions*, Harlow: Longman; and Markham, I. S., ed. (1996) *A World Religions Reader*, Oxford: Blackwell.

10   Morris, Desmond (1967) *The Naked Ape*, London: Corgi; Morris, Desmond
     (1969) *The Human Zoo*, London: Corgi.
11   E.g. Comfort, A. (1950) *Sexual Behaviour in Society*, London: Duckworth.
12   Morris, *The Naked Ape*, p. 9.
13   Sartre, Jean-Paul (1957) *Being and Nothingness*, London: Methuen.
14   Ayer, A. J. (1936) *Language, Truth and Logic*, p. 125. London: Victor
     Gollancz.
15   Ibid., pp. 5–16.
16   See Skinner, B. F. (1978) *Reflections on Behaviourism and Society*,
     Englewood Cliffs, NJ: Prentice-Hall.
17   Cf. Race, Alan (1983) *Christians and Religious Pluralism*, London: SCM. For
     a critical discussion of the typology see Markham, I. S. (January 1993) *New
     Blackfriars*, pp. 33–41.
18   Cantwell Smith, W. (1978) *The Meaning and End of Religion*, London:
     SPCK.

3

A cloud of witnesses

Theology begins with reflection on pastoral need under God in an ever-developing tradition. But how does this reflection take place? Upon what resources does it draw? Christianity has invariably given two broad answers to such questions, which have drawn on two distinct sources. The first source is 'internal' and focuses on Scripture and Christian tradition. The second is 'external' in that it draws widely on non-Christian material. In this chapter we will consider the former and in the next the latter.

The nature and use of the Bible

The Bible is the story of an ongoing historical drama which is set between creation and the Kingdom of God. The reason for this is that both Judaism and Christianity understand linear history to be the principal source of their knowledge of God. Old Testament Judaism, in particular, fostered a central respect for historical learning as the means whereby God's purposes for his chosen people were revealed. The knowledge of the past contained the key to understanding God's purposes for the future and it was sufficient to enable total obedience to them. The Christian understanding of the knowledge of God is broadly identical to this. As a religion of the messianic present, Christianity became the dénouement of the older Jewish expectation. Ironically, with the failure of the expected return of the Lord in glory, early Christianity also came to understand ongoing history as the arena in which God's purposes are worked out. Such fundamental elements of the Judaeo-Christian understanding of God are, as we shall see, as important to pastoral as they are to other branches of Christian theology. However, before we examine them we first need to consider some basic issues relating to the use of the Bible.

Protestantism, as is well known, has set the Bible over and against the Church and the world. The Reformers in general, and Luther in particular, used the biblical text as the source of the authority they required to challenge the prevailing authority of a Church which appeared to them to be worldly, all powerful and over coercive. Although the contingencies of the Reformation have long passed, the style of use of the biblical text which the Reformers championed has largely remained. It now exists in many different forms along a spectrum reaching from literal biblical fundamentalism at one end to the reflective and scholarly study of the Bible at the other. Although the term 'biblical fundamentalism' describes many positions, what they have in common is the belief that the biblical text has a final and self-sufficient authority. So understood, the modern world must never be placed above the biblical text, nor it seems even alongside it. James Barr describes such a position as having three characteristics:

> a) a very strong emphasis on the inerrancy of the Bible, the absence from it of any sort of error; b) a strong hostility to modern theology and to the results and implications of modern critical study of the Bible; c) an assumption that those who do not share this religious viewpoint are not really 'true Christians' at all.[1]

Barr also shows that such fundamentalism has taken many forms both intellectually and organizationally. It is, moreover, a common and recently somewhat revived feature of the way Christians understand the Bible. That revival has often taken place when biblical fundamentalists have come into, for them, congenial alliance with moral and often political conservatives. Such an understanding of the Bible needs to be questioned for a number of reasons, including the following.

The first reason why extreme biblical fundamentalism should be questioned concerns its subjection of modernity to the biblical text. It judges, for example, all forms of modern biblical scholarship as being inappropriate, in principle, to biblical study. This view also exists in attenuated forms, some of which tolerate forms of biblical criticism, providing they do not violate certain fundamental presuppositions about the inerrancy of the text itself. It is not necessary to defend the correctness, or otherwise, of all forms of biblical criticism to see that, as a modern intellectual discipline of at least two centuries in the making, it has brought immense benefits to our understanding of the biblical text and that it may be expected to continue to do so. As we learn more about the sources the biblical writers used in their work, as well as more about the way in which they used and adapted them for their purpose, so too we learn more about the meaning of the text for ourselves.

The second reason why biblical fundamentalism needs to be questioned is, ironically, because it displays a quality of mind which is notably absent from the biblical text itself. It is worth remembering that the Bible was some fourteen hundred years or more in the making and that, consequently, its many traditions were drawn from diverse historical and cultural periods. The often rough and ready way in which they are compiled means that traditions which do not cohere with each other often exist side by side. All this creates a wealth of diversity and tension within the biblical text itself. This is as evident in the New Testament as it is in the Old. Both show a rich and unfolding tradition in which freedom of presentation and interpretation is more evident than slavish conformity to the authority of previous writings. Of course, there was conformity on certain fundamental facts and their interpretation, but that did not compromise creativity, as we shall later see in some detail. Setting the whole of the biblical text against modernity, as fundamentalism does, runs counter to the nature of the text itself, and in particular to the way in which its later writers treated earlier ones either by adapting or even ignoring parts of them.

A third reason why biblical fundamentalism should be questioned can be drawn from the first two; it concerns its devaluation of modern experience. It is our lot, pastorally and ethically, to experience difficulties and problems which are either not mentioned in the biblical text at all or, if they are, appear to be in disagreement with it. As we wrestle with pastoral and ethical problems in, say, the nuclear and life sciences, we have to come to terms with facts and related issues which are not mentioned in the biblical text and if they are, but obliquely so. Not to wrestle with them is to disregard dangerously the actual circumstances of our contemporary pastoral and ethical dilemmas. It also marks a refusal by us to work out our salvation in fear and trembling as the biblical writers themselves did and encouraged their readers to do. In what follows, it will be presumed that the biblical faith, to coin a phrase, 'is still in the making'. Presumed, that is, that our strivings are like those of the people who wrote the Bible. With them we labour this side of the Kingdom of God and that alone is enough to create a common purpose and spirit between us and them. The dynamic creativity of the biblical faith continues in the present as, with new insights and experiences, we reflect on the meaning of older traditions in the light of ever-changing circumstances.

It has, however, been argued that the world of the Bible and our world are so different that any common understanding between them is difficult, if not downright impossible.[2] If this is the case, then all that we have been advocating will be impossible. Whilst it is, of course, undoubtedly the case that the modern world or worlds (it is doubtful if we can any longer talk of one world outlook) are very different from the biblical ones, it does not follow that they are different in every way. Our world is different in the obvious sense that we are influenced by science and its technologies and by subsequent discoveries in geometry, physics, astronomy and psychology, which have long replaced previous understandings of these subjects. Indeed, we are today more attuned to accepting 'paradigm shifts' of understanding which are made necessary by continuously revised knowledge and insight as well as by our incessant desire to understand them. We accept the fact, that is, that some of our most cherished understandings frequently have to change. Important similarities, however, between our world and the biblical worlds remain. What may be described as matters of the heart, rather than those of the intellect, remain noticeably the same. Matters of life and death; of love and hate; of wisdom and foolishness; of trust and suspicion; of fear and confidence, all these have about them a timeless resonance which is what enables us to understand references to them in the biblical text. In this way, when we study the biblical text (as when we study a present culture other than our own) we participate in something like a 'community of consciousness' in which by dint of our human nature we discover a resonance between our experience and that of others, however differently they may, at times, be expressed. These brief remarks belie, of course, the complexity of such a consciousness and we will later consider this in more detail, but they at least serve to show that there is every reason why we should believe there exists a common human experience which transcends history and culture. The notion of a 'community of consciousness' not only refers to our understanding of the relationship of the past with the present, it helps, further, with the discharge of our obligations to the future. We are now increasingly conscious of this as we wrestle with the incredibly stark implications of the effect of our lifestyle on the planet and its resources. We now turn, in the light of these introductory remarks, to a more detailed consideration of the significance of the biblical text for pastoral theology.

The Old Testament

In Israelite religion God is one, holy and righteous, and these attributes are inseparable. All nature and history are subject to God's sovereign lordship. Israel is in a covenant relationship with Yahweh (Exod 6.7) and all human beings are created in God's image (Ps 119.33–35). This means that the personal holiness of individuals is a reflection of divine holiness. The Psalmist graphically describes this as showing that the goodness of the Lord is to be seen in the land of the living (Ps 27.13). This gives rise to the pursuit of justice, righteousness and benevolence, and the view that there is a unity between the knowledge of God and the way of life it requires. This gives us the first and fundamental clue to the pastoral nature of the Old Testament.

Devotion to Yahweh and keeping his commandments constituted a way of life which led to happiness, security and prosperity. In all this, there was no distinction between the sacred and the secular. Every area of life and thought could be brought into harmony with the divine will. This is the theological background to the place of the Law in Israel's life, the main purpose of which was educative. The Law was not primarily to be understood as constraint or prohibition, but, rather as the means whereby every aspect of human life could be lived according to God's will in the assurance of the knowledge that this was achieved. In Israel, it was Law which provided the mediation between the holiness of God, personal holiness and the holiness of the nation. All this was and remains a source of great delight in Israel and is the reason why obedience to the Law was considered as joy rather than obligation because of the freedom it wrought. So understood, the religious life of Israel was and remains profoundly pastoral. Indeed, the profundity with which it is so, frequently escapes the understanding of Christians in general, and perhaps Protestant ones in particular. How, they ask, can a religion of law compare with the freedom bestowed by a religion of grace and forgiveness? The plain fact was that it did and still does for orthodox Jewish believers. Not to recognize this is to overlook the fundamental sense in which the religion of Israel is a profound source for pastoral theology. So much so that the administrators of the Law were themselves seen as pastoral figures. Their functions changed through the centuries, although the purpose of their work remained remarkably the same. In the long period of the Law's oral prehistory its keepers would have been those who exercised discipline and tradition in the nomadic communities. After the Settlement following c. 1020 BCE, and the remarkably rapid, in historical terms, establishment of the monarchy and cultic temple worship in Israel, the administration of the Law became the prerogative of priests. Yet later, after the Exile, rabbis became the teachers and custodians of the legal traditions and they remain so to this day.

Two further institutions of Israelite religion should be noticed for their pastoral significance: the Prophets and the Teachers of Wisdom. Compared with the antiquity of Law in Israel's life, prophecy made a late appearance. It was possibly Syrian in origin and did not flourish in Israel until the eighth century BCE. The later ascriptions of the title prophet to: Abraham (Gen 20.7); Moses (Deut 18.15); Aaron (Exod 7.1) and Miriam (Exod 15.20) are a later reading back of a new institution into the older tradition where it originally had no place. The Prophets were not, as such, opposed to the Law and its cult. What they sought was essentially the same: personal and corporate holiness. Their protest against the Law arose because they believed it was no longer achieving this. The background to prophecy lay in the inexorable urbanization and formalization of Israel's life and religion in the centuries following the Settlement. Along with this went a willingness to accept syncretistic religious practices, as happened when the Baal religions of Caanan continued to elicit occasional devotion thereby refusing to be displaced entirely by the insurgent Yahwism. Here again, we touch upon a much debated historical question concerning the Settlement itself. Did it in fact occur at all? Or, if it did was it anything like the popular imagination as instructed by tradition supposed? If it did occur, was it as complete as Israel's later historians claimed that it was? Whatever the answer to these questions, we certainly know that: (a) religion in Israel and the keeping of the Law became, for many, essentially a cultic and less life-pervading matter, and; (b) that there was a widespread belief that worship of Yahweh and Baal were not incompatible. Hence, the prophetic protest.

Prophets were women and men under calling. Their office was not inherited, as the priestly and levitical ones were. The calling came only from Yahweh and response to it put the prophets under an inescapable constraint to carry out their work, often against their own will. They required no special training and often, as did Amos, made much of the fact that they had not received any (Amos 7.14). The prophetic message, in its many forms, sought to restore both individual and collective righteousness in Israel, especially when it was perceived to be threatened. Initially, at least, it took the form of judgement in which the wrath of a righteous Yahweh sought to punish Israel for its laxity and waywardness. Amos, for example, proclaimed a radical message of social justice which he derived from his vision of the utter righteousness and sovereign lordship of Yahweh, not only over Israel, but also over the surrounding nations and even over the natural order itself. Amos' vision of the universality of Yahweh's righteous sovereignty stood as a counter to self-satisfied cultic laxity and the religious syncretism and economic exploitation which often went with it. He achieved this by showing the all-pervading nature of Yahweh's righteousness and by detailing at length its requirements in specific areas of Israel's life such as economics, housing, trade, labour and international affairs. Amos was convinced that Israel could not escape the impending divine punishment for its transgressions (Amos 2.12–16). 'Fallen, no more to rise, is maiden Israel; forsaken on her land, with no one to raise her up' (Amos 5.2). From all this there will be no escape (Amos 9.1–4). The threat of punishment is made the more poignant because of the covenant relationship Israel had with Yahweh, 'You only have I known of all the families of the earth' (Amos 3.2a). The tenderness of this relationship makes the wrath of the punishment the more excruciating. Amos does turn his thoughts to the future of Israel after its punishment, but he is not optimistic about it. Some, a remnant, may be left (Amos 9.12), but if so it will be a punished, shaken and contrite remnant which may live to see the fallen Israel restored, but of that there could be no assurance. Whether this hope for the future was an original part of Amos' message, is debated. It is certainly not in tune with his former unqualified warnings about judgement and doom, but as it stands the book ends on an optimistic note which looks forward to the restoration of Israel's fortunes.

Hosea was more directly concerned with Israel's syncretism, and Isaiah inveighs against its mistaken attempts to place confidence in military alliances rather than in Yahweh, but they both echoed the pastoral imperative of Amos' message and desired to restore the lost spirituality of Israel and thereby the political and economic well-being of its people. Brief consideration of the writings of just one more prophet will further illustrate the, for our purposes important, fact that prophecy in Israel arose from a profoundly pastoral motivation making it a significant part of the biblical contribution to pastoral theology.

Jeremiah flourished at the time when the Babylonian armies surrounded Jerusalem in 586 BCE. The then king, Zedekiah, sought Jeremiah's advice and received it immediately. 'You shall be handed over to the king of Babylon' (Jer 37.17). Israel's transgressions had been so great that the final exile was imminent and unavoidable. It was in these adverse circumstances that Jeremiah exemplified himself as a political realist and pastoral visionary of the very first rank. He looked forward to a time when the Lord would make a new covenant with the house of Israel and the house of Judah (Jer 31.31), a covenant which would be written in their hearts (Jer 31.34). Because of this hope for the future, Jeremiah wrote to the Babylonian exiles urging them to settle where they were and build houses and live in them (Jer 29). They were then to await the restoration of their covenant relationship.

The point of the widespread prophetic emphasis on judgement was to stress the slender possibility that Israel could yet experience Yahweh's mercy and forgiveness. This was the pastoral goal which all the prophets sought in their different ways.

The third way in which the Old Testament can be seen as a resource for pastoral theology is to be found in its body of, so-called, Wisdom literature. This ranks in pastoral significance with that of the Law and the Prophets, but it has, popularly at least, received less attention. This literature consists of the books of Proverbs, Ecclesiastes, Job, The Song of Solomon, parts of Genesis, notably the Jacob saga, and some Psalms (e.g. Pss 1, 49, 78, 127). Couplets of wisdom are to be found in other Psalms (e.g. Pss 31.23, 34.5ff). In addition to the above, Wisdom writing is to be found in the Apocrypha which is the most well-known collection of such writing. 'Wisdom' in Israel was a form of experiential knowledge which could be used to practical benefit. It was an elementary attempt to master life by discerning some order behind the flux and ambiguity of natural events. Wisdom, as such, is anthropocentric rather than theocentric and in this it differs markedly from the other literatures of the Old Testament. What it teaches is discovered by experience rather than received in propositions and its authority is derived from the continued experience by which, in each generation, it is tested. The earliest wisdom traditions in Israel developed outside the other great institutions of Exodus, Covenant and Law. It is nonetheless extremely ancient in its origin and has many parallels in other ancient Near Eastern non-Jewish literatures. Recent scholarship has stressed the previously unappreciated extent and antiquity of much of Israel's Wisdom writing and shown how it was only brought into theological conformity with other traditions much later in Israel's history.[3]

Wisdom is invariably expressed in simple proverbial or narrative forms which are appropriate to its elementary nature. 'Proverb' is a word which is used to cover a wide range of Hebrew poetry and can mean a pointed saying; a taunt, or a curse; a figurative prophetic message; a parable as an extended proverb; a longer wisdom poem; or a sententious maxim of moral wisdom. All these literary forms of wisdom are suited to verbal transmission and they achieve this by appealing to the imagination. They are meant to be called to mind easily to serve as ever-ready guidelines amidst perplexity, temptation and confusion. 'The purpose which these maxims are intended to serve could be called, rather than teaching, an art for living or at least a certain technique for life.'[4] Wisdom discerned these maxims by way of its confidence in the divine presence in the natural order of things.[5] The task of wisdom is

> For learning about wisdom and instruction,
>> for understanding words of insight,
> for gaining instruction in wise dealing,
>> righteousness, justice, and equity;
> to teach shrewdness to the simple,
>> knowledge and prudence to the young –
> Let the wise also hear and gain in learning,
>> and the discerning acquire skill,
> to understand a proverb and a figure,
>> the words of the wise and their riddles. (Prov 1.2–6)

The practical issues which the Wisdom literature addresses include law and order (Prov 4.14–17); land possession (Prov 22.28); the poor (Prov 14.21, 15.25); the causes of poverty: idleness (Prov 6.6–11), idle pursuits (Prov 12.11), ignorance (Prov 13.18), wine-drinking (Prov 23.20–21); the pity of the needy as a divine service (Prov 19.17), which is paralleled by the words of Jesus in Matthew (25.31–46); the advantages of wealth as a means to power (Prov 14.20); and the causes of anger (Prov 16.32). Faithfulness in marriage and trustworthiness in friendship are commanded throughout. Evil is to be avoided (Prov 4.25–27), and love must have the courage to reprove if it is to have moral value (Prov 27.5). Sin is recognized as universal (Prov 20.9) and education and joyfulness are repeatedly encouraged. Even this brief survey of the specific concerns of the book of Proverbs shows what a profoundly pastoral literature it is.

The pastoral nature of the Wisdom literature is, of course, particularly evident in the book of Job. Job's plight, which focused on his suffering from undeserved punishment, is the basic theme of the narrative. The futility of sincere but mistaken explanations for it are exposed, Job seeks his solace in quietness and through that his confidence in the Lord remains. The pastoral significance of this book cannot be overestimated. It essays the so often inadequate nature of inter-human reaction in the face of tragedy and contrasts this with the profundity and infinite resourcefulness of the human–divine interaction. It marks the triumph of the human spirit over adversity and stands as probably the most profound biblical comment on how human life and dignity can be sustained amid tragedy.[6]

The diverse Wisdom traditions contain a mass of ordinary detailed reference to the actual circumstances of human suffering and confusion. For this reason alone, the study of them is essential to pastoral theology, as much for the importance of how they cope with adversity as for what they teach. They are to be read as compilations of the sayings of the wise, who were probably male and elderly. They may have lacked imagination at times, and also been pedantic, but the overall accumulation of wisdom they contain is an impressive achievement. We shall later see that the teaching of Jesus is being reinterpreted in the light of the Wisdom traditions of the Old Testament.

We have briefly considered how Israel's three great institutions of Law, Prophets and Wisdom, can all be studied for their pastoral, as well as for their historical and theological significance. Indeed, as we have seen throughout, they were universally motivated by a compassionate concern for the well-being of those they addressed. For that reason alone it can well be argued that the key to understanding these traditions lies more in the study of their pastoral aspirations than in it does in the other ways they can be read and interpreted. The literary form of these traditions may often be strange to us and their historical settings may be almost totally obscure, but their pastoral integrity and significance stands as something which illustrates the unity of religion with all aspects of life and morality. No detail is seemingly too small for attention and the pastoral concern of the writers is evident throughout. Indeed, as we saw in Chapter 1, such details not only set the agenda for the theological and pastoral response, they invariably had a direct effect upon its nature. Here again human need is seen throughout as the fundamental data from which theological insight and pastoral care is achieved.

The New Testament

We will now consider, briefly, the senses in which various New Testament books can be used as sources of pastoral theology. To place a necessary limit on the scope of such a study, we will confine our attention to the Synoptic Gospels (Matthew, Mark and Luke), the main Pauline epistles and the ministry of Jesus. These texts are probably the closest we have to the historical Jesus and some of the Pauline epistles are the earliest documents in the New Testament.

The Synoptic Gospels

We cannot be sure why the Gospels were written in the first place. It was certainly not for the posterity they have subsequently enjoyed. Their writers can only have had their immediate circumstances in mind when they wrote, although, as we shall see, there is good reason to think that St Luke's Gospel is something of an exception to this. There is only one place in the Gospels where there is anything like an allusion to the purpose of their being written: 'But these are written so that you may come to believe that Jesus is the Messiah, the Son of God, and that through believing you may have life in his name' (John 20.31). In order to enable belief in this way, of course, the writers of the Gospels had to address themselves to a range of issues and this they did with the needs of their readers very much in mind. Hence, pastoral considerations are again very much to the fore. So much so, in fact, that the meaning of any particular Gospel passage can often best be understood if we ask of it the simple question: what pastoral need or needs is the writer addressing?

The Gospels were not, of course, made up. They were all, rather, compiled from pre-existing oral and possibly some written traditions about Jesus. Redaction criticism now enables us to study the theology of the individual gospel writers (using also the tools of textual and historical criticism), by drawing attention to the ways the writers edited the pre-existing oral and written material at their disposal.[7] Such methods are applicable most easily to Matthew and Luke, but Mark and John may also be approached in this way. This compilation of previously existing traditions into Gospels was highly sophisticated, in the sense that it was a consciously purposive activity.

For our purposes we will consider only the three, so-called, 'Synoptic' Gospels: Mark, Matthew and Luke. This is not because the Gospel of John is any less pastorally significant, indeed it is redolent with pastoral concerns which relate to the establishment and maintenance of the Johannine faith communities. It is because that Gospel is so different from the other three that a number of preliminary considerations would have to be made prior to its study and these would detain us unnecessarily. The first three Gospels are called 'synoptic' because they all follow a similar outline of the life of Jesus. This is essentially because Matthew and Luke both follow Mark's outline, although they do so in their slightly different ways. Each of these Gospels is made up of separate *pericopae* (small passages and episodes) which are consciously arranged and set in a wider sustaining narrative. An analogy which well illustrates the way this was done is that of a string of different coloured beads. A good jeweller will not only select the beads for stringing carefully, she or he will also arrange their colour in an order which will maximise the overall final effect of the piece. A Gospel is very much like this. There is a thread running through and the different parts are consciously meant to be understood in relation to each other. The meaning of the parts is, therefore, to be understood by noticing their relationship to the whole. We will now explore something of the pastoral significance of all this by considering each of the Synoptic Gospels in turn.

Mark

Mark's Gospel was, in all probability, the first to be written. It appeared in Rome some time around 65–68 CE. It is the shortest of the Gospels and, theologically sophisticated though it is, it is the least literary of them all, being written in a common Greek style. The theological sophistication of the Gospel, however, is in marked contrast to this and can be discovered, in particular, from considering the ordering of the material within it, as suggested above. What becomes immediately obvious is that this order is conscious and purposive. The confession of Peter (8.29) is pivotal. Before this, Jesus' ministry is a secret affair and after it he begins his public progress to Jerusalem and crucifixion. Why did Jesus first keep his identity secret in this way? Is it even correct to suppose that he did so at all? Or, is this so-called 'Messianic Secret' an invention of the writer of the Gospel? We cannot be sure about the answers to these questions and scholarly opinion is, not unusually, divided.[8] But we do know that Mark must have had a purpose in writing as he did. Could it be that Christians in Rome, some thirty years after the crucifixion, were puzzled that contemporaries of Jesus did not recognize Jesus' messiahship when they met him? A concern such as this would certainly have been enough to motivate Mark to write as he did, thereby showing his readers the lack of recognition was according to Jesus' own express wishes whilst he instructed his disciples. Another pastoral motivation behind the Gospel is Mark's consistent attention to the place of suffering in the Christian life. Indeed, it is here that we encounter the pastoral heart of his writing. When the Gospel was written, Christians in Rome were already suffering from the horrific Neronian persecutions particularly when they were held responsible for causing the fire which destroyed much of Rome in 64 CE. Mark responded by showing that Jesus also suffered and, moreover, that he was fully aware that he would do so before it happened. In this way Mark suggests that suffering is part of the divine plan and that there must be a period of persecution before the return of the Lord in glory. The agony and confusion this causes is inescapable and is the object of his pastoral concern.

The Gospel ends with Mary Magdalene, Mary the mother of James, and Salome at the tomb being afraid, and this is notoriously difficult to interpret. It may well be that Mark 16.9–20 is a later addition to the Gospel, but if so it would contain no mention of the resurrection. 'So they went out and fled from the tomb, for terror and amazement had seized them; and they said nothing to anyone, for they were afraid' (Mark 16.8). Dare we suppose that Mark is leaving the reader with the realization that fear has been a feature of following Jesus from the beginning? This theme can be traced throughout the Gospel where apprehension, confusion and fear are commonly portrayed among the disciples. They followed him in amazement, misunderstanding and even fear.

The theme of this Gospel is, therefore, that of following Jesus.[9] Mark wrote in ways which clearly enabled his readers to do this, particularly when they were experiencing perplexity, fear and suffering. Considered in this way, Mark's Gospel can be seen to have been written consciously to meet, and to meet pastorally, the very real needs and concerns of its readers. Instances of explicit instruction and teaching in the Gospel can all be seen to be given to help its readers meet their pressing pastoral needs as well as prepare for the return of the Lord in glory. All this was very much instruction for the moment, rather than the recording of timeless pastoral and other truths for posterity. The Gospel stands, however, as a source of inspiration to Christians of all ages who, for whatever reason, suffer for their faith. Again it is necessary for our purpose only that we notice its profoundly pastoral nature through the way in which the writer is consciously working with the pastoral needs of his readers in mind.

Matthew

The Gospel of Matthew is very different from that of Mark, both in style and purpose, but again we may observe that its writing was prompted in the first place, in part at least, by pastoral concern. Like Mark, Matthew wants his readers to follow Jesus, but he wants them to do so in a particular way and for a specific purpose. This way, for Matthew, is the way of *righteousness* (Matt 5.20). Righteousness, its nature and purpose, is thus a central theme of the Gospel. Above all, readers of the Gospel are enjoined to be righteous for a particular reason: that they may enter the Kingdom of Heaven (Matt 5.17–20). Significantly, the parable of the unforgiving servant (Matt 18.23–35) is without parallel in Mark or Luke. It starkly portrays the consequences for any who fail to fulfil the righteous demands of the Gospel. In the record of Jesus' baptism by John, Matthew records that Jesus submitted to it in the first place because he wanted 'to fulfil all righteousness' (Matt 3.15). Perhaps Matthew's interest in righteousness arose because, unlike Mark, he did not expect the imminent return of the Lord in glory (Matt 25.1–13). Matthew has some vision of an intervening period in which lives had to be ordered before the Lord returned in glory and in which believers had to spend the time wisely preparing for entry into the Kingdom of Heaven when the opportunity for it occurred. The beatitudes (Matt 5.3–12) are congratulations to people in their present condition, made necessary because assurances were, no doubt, earnestly sought by Christian believers as to whether or not they were doing the right thing to entitle them to entry into the Kingdom.

Matthew more readily addresses himself to ongoing concerns than Mark. Examples are wrongdoing and its consequences (Matt 18.15–18), and the mitigation of Mark's seeming prohibition of divorce or, at least, the right to remarry after it (Matt 19.19). In the light of all this, Matthew's stress throughout the Gospel on the nature of the righteousness which is sufficient for salvation would thus have been keenly read. He also notes, incidentally, that there is a higher righteousness (Matt 19.16–22) which is achieved by some, but which is not necessary for all. The writer, or writers, of Matthew's Gospel are thus deeply sensitive to the readers' insecurity about salvation, to such an extent that this may be seen as a theme which is fundamental to the purpose of the whole Gospel. The more so, because it was written for readers whose Christian faith was very close to Judaism, unlike the markedly more gentile Christians for whom Mark and Luke wrote. Concern for righteousness is a traditional Jewish preoccupation which was, as we saw, formerly met by the assurance and delight provided by the Law. With that taken away, or at least clearly qualified (Matt 5.20) what assurance was there of salvation? Matthew's answer is clear and resonant; seek righteousness and practise its virtues: alms giving, prayer and fasting are accordingly enjoined throughout the Gospel. As with the Gospel of Mark, there is, of course, much more of pastoral significance in Matthew's Gospel than these few remarks can indicate, but, again, they simply show that running through the many other purposes the Gospel might have had there is a prominent pastoral concern which, in all likelihood, largely motivated the writing of the Gospel in the first place.

Luke

Luke's Gospel is markedly different from the other two Synoptics. The main difference is that, unlike them, it has a sequel: the Acts of the Apostles. There is, further, a marked difference in its treatment of the delay of the coming of Jesus in glory. Luke clearly expects the return of the Lord, but he is reconciled to its probably indefinite delay. Rather like latter-day main-stream Christianity, Luke knows that Christian life has to come to terms with the ostensible permanence of history. The main reason for this is that this Gospel was probably the latest to be written and may well date from the beginning of the second century. As would therefore be expected, we find in Luke's Gospel a concern with the ordering of daily life (e.g. Luke 12.35–38). This is also clear from the more central place the Gospel gives to instruction on ethical issues as such in comparison with the other two Synoptics, although, as we have seen, Matthew moves partly away from Mark also in this direction. For example, Luke introduces an ethical element into the teaching of John the Baptist, whose hearers' first question is 'What then should we do?' (Luke 3.10). The 'good' in Luke's Gospel is invariably recognizable as an ethical concept (Luke 23.50, Acts 11.24) and saintliness has an ethical perspective (Acts 3.14, 16.6, 20.26). In his beautiful attempt to tell the whole story of Christianity from the beginning to when Paul preached the gospel in Rome openly and unhindered, Luke traces the emergence of the Christian 'way' of life as a distinctive expression of Christianity. By the time Luke's Gospel was written, Christians in Rome were again suffering persecution and Luke, as Mark did before him, exhorts his readers to endure their suffering steadfastly. The Christian way of life is not here commended as an imitation of Jesus, or an imitation of any of his immediate followers, Luke is more concerned to explore the meaning of the Christian way of life in the now changed circumstances of his readers. Real treasure is what abides (Luke 12.33) and it is worth possessing for its own sake (Luke 12.34) rather than (as for Matthew) because it leads to entry into the Kingdom of Heaven. Luke is, clearly, preparing his readers to live the Christian life indefinitely in the world as they know it and encouraging them to consider that life as a dispensation following the 'mid point in time' (of Jesus), which was preceded by the Old Testament.[10]

These brief remarks on the Synoptic Gospels have been intended to show that the use to which they can be put in the study of pastoral theology must include the study of their central pastoral nature and purpose. They were written, as we have seen, with a particular readership in mind. We know this because of the sensitivity all the writers show for them. Indeed, they may well have lived among those for whom they wrote and shared in the anxieties they addressed. What they all show is a fundamental pastoral concern for the spiritual and earthly welfare of their readers.

The historical Jesus

Reflect though we can in these ways about the place of the study of Jesus in pastoral theology, we cannot avoid also reflecting on the very real critical question about whether it is possible to know anything about the historical Jesus at all. Or, at least, know enough about him in sufficient detail to construct a pastoral theology. The problem arises from the distinction between the 'Jesus of history' and the 'Christ of faith'. The two are not identical as we can see from discrepant, some of them considerably so, accounts of Jesus in the Gospels. This distinction is effectively the story of nineteenth- and, particularly, twentieth-century Gospel scholarship.[11] Although some progress has been made, it is a story which is still incomplete and will probably remain so. It is possible, of course, to ignore such critical questions and treat the texts of the Gospels on their face value, but we have already considered why this is not acceptable.

The biblical scholar and theologian Rudolf Bultmann pointed out the unlikelihood of us ever being certain that we have reliable historical information about Jesus. Bultmann did not question that the historical event of Jesus stood behind the Gospels. What he did question was any claim that we have ready access to it. His own famous 'solution' was to claim that the only way in which we can avail ourselves of the significance of Jesus' ministry and teaching is for us to 'demythologize' the Gospels, so that we might discover the *kerygma*, the essential 'grace and event' of the saving power of Jesus to which the reader can respond. The critical discussion which this view provoked was immense. In many ways, it has been the agenda of much post-war Gospel study. For our purpose, it is interesting to note its outlines. Bultmann repeatedly points out that the original message of Jesus, and also original historical information about his ministry, is not available to us, since 'the message of Jesus is a presupposition for the theology of the New Testament, rather than a part of that theology itself'.[12] He put it in another way when he said that 'Jesus the proclaimer became the proclaimed'.[13] He rejected a view which is often put forward to counter this: that we can know about Jesus' message because it was essentially about love. Love, he claimed, is not a principle from which specific and universally applicable norms can be derived.[14] In the 1950s Bultmann's pupils, among them Käsemann, Fuchs and Bornkamm, expressed the view that while Bultmann's methods may have been correct, the conclusions he drew from them may not be. One result of all this was the appearance of Bornkamm's *Jesus of Nazareth* in 1956. He concludes the first chapter of this by saying that '. . . the primitive tradition of Jesus is brim full of history.'[15] Such a claim may be thought to be something of an overreaction against the so-called Bultmannian scepticism, but it did much to generate what has been called the 'New Quest' for the historical Jesus. This still continues, as research attempts to press back through the Gospel records to some knowledge of the historical Jesus, however tentative and incomplete it may be.[16]

This debate is important for our purpose, since no claims about the significance of the historical Jesus for pastoral theology should be made unless they have been made subject to its strictures. We were left at least with a haunting impression of the strangeness of Jesus, a fact which was noticed by Schweitzer at the beginning of the twentieth century.[17] On this view, which we will see below is now being challenged, all Jesus' teaching and pastoral actions were not only influenced by, they were also bound up with and part of, his radical expectation of the imminence of the Kingdom of God. To the extent in which this remains true of our knowledge of Jesus it explains, at least in part, why we cannot derive from it a complete account of a pastoral ministry which is binding and definitive for all time. Any more, that is, than we can read off from it a complete account of morality which will settle all questions for all time. All this is not to say that study of the person of Jesus in the Gospels is not crucially important to pastoral theology and ethics. It is but to say that such study must be subject to the constraints and findings of critical scholarship.

Notwithstanding the magisterial influence on modern scholarship about Jesus which was exercised by Bultmann and his pupils, who all held in one way or another that the essence of Jesus' message was eschatological, a considerable amount of recent New Testament scholarship has, once again, been trying to get behind the New Testament narratives in order to identify and reinterpret things he did and said. This scholarship is in effect, distinct from the so-called 'New Quest' for the historical Jesus which was championed by Bultmann's pupils Käsemann, Fuchs and Bornkamm. They did not demur from the teacher's methods. They simply reapplied them and came to somewhat less negative conclusions than he did. More recent scholars are breaking from these methods and turning more to those used in the study of comparative history, the history of religions, cultural anthropology and the social sciences.[18] The results they have achieved are already impressive, but they should, perhaps, be tempered with a familiar caution. Each 'age' of Jesus scholarship has, by dint of the fact that it has used its own, and therefore contemporary methods, discovered something new about him. What, therefore, all such new methods have in common is that they see a Jesus who is a reflection of their own modernity. This is, however, no reason for not attempting such scholarship, providing we are mindful of this its perennial limitation. More positively, we can interpret the fact that this invariably happens as testimony to the enduring fascination every age has with the person of Jesus. In what follows we will illustrate some of the findings of this more recent Jesus scholarship for pastoral theology.

The most pastorally important feature of the new emergent picture of Jesus is that he appears more as a teacher of wisdom than as only a strange eschatological prophet. The many different types of Wisdom teachers of the Old Testament, drew, as we have seen, on accumulated wisdom which was capable of being known by everyone. They pointed out, that is, what was self-evidently the case in easily memorable forms. Jesus, we can now see, did this by illuminating the deeper meaning of commonplace wisdom and everyday incidents. Such deeper meaning had two consistent features throughout his teaching. First, it pointed to a more profound knowledge of God than his hearers apparently possessed as well as to what that knowledge required of those who then acquired it. Second, this knowledge and the action it required was invariably subversive of established norms and received wisdom, particularly those represented by the various religious establishments of his day. In all this Jesus was not consciously building religious, even new religious, communities. All that was to come later, particularly, as we shall see, in the work and writings of St Paul. Jesus was undoubtedly preparing his hearers for the Kingdom which was to come, but he was doing it in a way which enabled them to live in the present in the face of all its pressing demands. At this point, the new Jesus scholarship raises an interesting question which New Testament scholars will no doubt have to address. Namely, were Jesus' immediate followers more expectant of the imminence of his Kingdom than he was? If so, their successors who did address themselves to understanding the meaning of his message for a more permanent and ongoing world might have been less innovative than they have recently been thought to be. Perhaps, after all, they were rediscovering something essential about Jesus' original message which their immediate predecessors had overlooked. Continuing Jesus scholarship will, no doubt, throw light on this intriguing possibility.

One of the most influential of the recent reinterpreters of the ministry of Jesus is John Dominic Crossan. In *The Historical Jesus: The Life of a Mediterranean Jewish Peasant*, he rejects entirely all Bultmannian and other attempts to interpret Jesus' ministry eschatologically, in similarity with that of John the Baptist, and emphasizes the way in which Jesus' teaching was all aimed at enabling his followers to live in the present. In proof of this, he claims that Jesus' life and teaching must be understood in the context of contemporary Judaism.[19] Crossan believes that it is possible to identify in the New Testament those sayings which go back to Jesus and to derive from them a portrait which is different from that given in prevailing New Testament scholarship. Jesus, according to Crossan, did have a social vision at the heart of which was a conviction that the divine presence permeated all human affairs. He describes Jesus as 'a peasant Jewish cynic' whose 'strategy, implicitly for himself and explicitly for his followers, was the combination of *free healing and common eating*, a religious and economic egalitarianism that negated alike and at once the hierarchical and patronal normalcies of Jewish religion and Roman power'.[20] The Jesus that emerges from Crossan's study negates what he finds, not because he wants to point away from the world, but because he wants to show an alternative way of living within it. The implications of this and similar developments in contemporary Jesus scholarship for pastoral theology are obvious. Here is a Jesus who takes minute cognizance of and care for the actual circumstances in which his followers find themselves by repeatedly showing that the presence of God was obscured rather than revealed by both Jewish religion and Roman polity. Little wonder, given this interpretation of what Jesus said and did, that the two institutions he attacked eventually and to their mutual convenience, conspired against him to death. Crossan's scholarship is awesome in the detail about contemporary life in Palestine it cites to support this radical reinterpretation of Jesus and it will undoubtedly continue to exercise the considerable influence in Jesus studies which it has already established. The ensuing debate will be a crucial one for pastoral theologians and all who seek to understand anything of the relevance of the ministry of Jesus to the modern world. It will undoubtedly still be as disturbing of received wisdom and vested interest as it was in the first place.

We will now reflect a little on the pastoral significance of understanding Jesus as a subversive teacher of wisdom in this way. Most importantly for our purpose, Jesus always seemed well aware of the fact that his teaching would cause puzzlement and often downright bewilderment. This is no doubt why he often followed it up by some further teaching or action which was meant by way of explanation. This is more the method of a patient teacher and pastor than one that would be expected of an eschatological prophet. It is as though, time after time in his teaching, by both deed and word, he seems to anticipate the confusion and instinctively know what to do to help dispel it. Let just two illustrations of this suffice. The parable of the sower in Mark 4.1-20 and its Matthean and Lukean parallels, uniquely contains an explanation which was called for because the disciples failed to understand its meaning when first told. The writer of Mark's Gospel uses this to illustrate his theme of the secret messiahship of Jesus and the other Gospel writers followed him even though they did not pursue the theme of secrecy in the same way. This and all the parables well illustrate what we have seen to be pastorally important about Jesus' teaching; the way he gains insight out of the commonplace. Mark relates the parable and the incident of its telling to the way Jesus was instructing his disciples into a secret wisdom which was deliberately concealed from the masses from whom the explanation was withheld (Mark 4.11). Here even the everyday and the seemingly self-evident fail to bring understanding without explanation. Here too we find a disturbing message; much religiosity is transient and barren and in making this point the parable points to deeper and perennially relevant truths about the need to avoid the temptations of prosperity and those created by difficulties and persecutions. This parable and the setting of its telling contains a wisdom which is of far wider significance than would be indicated by its interpretation as only an eschatological warning. Indeed, fitting the parables, generally, into an eschatological straitjacket can easily cause us to overlook their deeper pastoral profundity.[21]

A second example of Jesus acting out of a seemingly pastoral motive to dispel confusion can also be found in Mark's Gospel. Mark records Jesus as predicting his passion three times (Mark 8.31, 9.31, 10.33–34), and each time he shows that this caused perplexity for those who heard the predictions just as it no doubt did for his readers. Mark records what Jesus said in reply each time: 'For those who want to save their life will lose it, and those who lose their life for my sake, and for the sake of the gospel, will save it' (Mark 8.35); 'Whoever wants to be first must be last of all and servant of all' (Mark 9.35); this is repeated in chapter 10 with the additional saying about 'The Son of Man came not to be served but to serve, and to give his life a ransom for many' (Mark 10.45). This thrice repeated theme makes a clear general point. Suffering is an inescapable part of the Christian life and to follow Jesus it is necessary to follow in his suffering. Again in each instance we find examples of radically subversive teaching which might have been constructed by Mark but which, equally, might also point back to Jesus' definitive style.

One could go on from such a brief study to reflect on the pastoral nature of the detailed accounts of Jesus' ministry and teaching. But here it is only possible to mention them briefly. These accounts have to be interpreted in the light of the varying pictures of Jesus which are presented by the Gospel writers.

Jesus preached a radical message of the Kingdom which required repentance (Mark 1.14). This repentance was for sinfulness and it required singleness of mind and purpose, in preparation for entry into what some, at least, though to be the imminently expected Kingdom. Specific pastoral matters are discussed in this context: about marriage and divorce, about dealing with children, about service to others, about the bereaved, the sick, the poor and the outcast. Jesus is portrayed not as a teacher laying down hard and fast rules for all to follow in every circumstance, but as one who sounded a watchword to be remembered whenever his hearers decided to do anything. He, invariably, refused to excuse those he met from taking responsibility for their own beliefs and conduct. Much of his teaching prompted questions and he frequently replied to them with further ones. Such oblique methods enabled Jesus to inculcate a sense of self-realization and awareness in others. He achieved this largely in the course of everyday contact with the people he met. His style repeatedly created some lasting insight out of an ordinary experience or event. In fact, his ministry was noted for its ordinariness, as was his appearance (so much a problem, as we have seen, for the next generation of his followers). He sought the company of 'publicans and sinners'. 'These were not just people who ritually sinned, but were persons of immoral life, of proven dishonesty or followers of suspected or degraded occupations.'[22] Indeed, Jesus' marked preference was for the company of sinners who had repented since they provided the model for others to follow.[23] All the Gospel traditions record information about Jesus' contact with sinners. Repeatedly, it is the very presence of Jesus, his closeness, which was the means of forgiveness and acceptance. Indeed, it is also the sinners who are shown as recognizing, before others, who Jesus really was.

The subversion of traditional spirituality and morality could hardly be more dramatic than this. The shock and confusion, we now might think, it deliberately caused is a recurrent theme throughout the Gospels. When Jesus' ministry is seen in this way it comes as little surprise that it was left to others to describe his person as 'prophet', 'priest', 'king', 'saviour' and 'messiah'. His description of himself was that of a Shepherd (Luke 12.32). He speaks to a throng because they are like sheep without a shepherd (Mark 6.34). In Matthew (15.24), dealing with the dispute with the disciples about whether he should heal the daughter of the Canaanite woman, Jesus replies 'I was sent only to the lost sheep of the house of Israel'. This is an intriguing saying which probably dates back to a view of Jesus' work before the Gentile Mission which followed the first Apostolic Council in Jerusalem in 49 CE. In Luke 12.32 he refers to his disciples as 'little flock'. Most powerfully, we get Jesus' quotation from Zechariah in Mark 14.27, where he predicts on the Mount of Olives that they (his followers) will all fall away; for it is written, 'I will strike the shepherd, and the sheep will be scattered'. Recognition of the subversive emphasis in the ministry of Jesus undoubtedly helps us to understand something of the force of such otherwise strange sayings. We now turn to a consideration of the place of pastoral concerns in the writings and ministry of St Paul.

Paul

St Paul helped to transform an originally Jewish form of Christianity into a faith which became open to Gentiles and thereby potentially a world religion. He was, as James Dunn has reminded us in a major new study, 'undoubtedly the *first* Christian theologian'.[24] Interestingly, Dunn draws attention to the continuity between Paul's teaching on the Law and that of Judaism. By contrast most commentators stress discontinuity at this point. Dunn writes, 'Paul's critique of the law was primarily directed against its abuse by sin, and against his fellow kinsfolk's assumption that the law's protection continued to give them before God a distinctive and favoured position over that of other nations.'[25] Whatever the detail of Paul's stance on this he has certainly been, arguably, the most abiding influence on the subsequent nature of Christian thought and practice. So many of the things we take for granted about the pastoral nature of Christian theology, as we shall see, do not pre-date Paul. He created them in the often turbulent circumstances out of which the earliest Christian communities came. Indeed, many of his epistles came into existence because of disputes which had broken out, often between Paul himself and the earliest Christian communities as well as between strong personalities within them. In all this, he was the architect of Christianity, in the sense that he erected on the foundations of the new faith in Jesus systems of ecclesial organization, ministry and theology which became, even in his own lifetime, the standards of emerging Christian orthodoxy. And they have effectively remained so ever since. Without his work, in all its diversity, it is even possible to doubt if Christianity would have survived at all. Indeed, to the extent in which the Gentile Mission was of his personal creation this claim is self-evident, since the alternative form of Jewish Christianity not only lost out against it, it also ceased to exist after a very short period. We will consider more of these things below and mention them here only to illustrate, by way of introduction, the truly awesome nature of Paul's achievements.

The sources for our knowledge of this achievement are his own writings and Luke's Acts of the Apostles. There are notoriously difficult questions to answer about relating these two sources, because of the incomplete and sometimes contradictory information they contain. Nor is there any mention in the Acts of the Apostles that Paul ever wrote any letters. We shall not consider this problem, beyond observing that the purposes of St Paul's writings and those of Luke in Acts are very different, and this is largely why the two narratives are difficult to reconcile with each other. Paul wrote his letters for specific purposes to identifiable groups and individuals. Luke, as the historian of the early Church, was writing to show his Roman patron both how Christianity came about and why Rome had nothing to fear from it (Luke 1.1ff). Our remarks will be based on Paul's own writings. Hence the first question is, which of the many books ascribed to him in the New Testament are authentically his? Arguable though it may be, we shall presume that Colossians, Ephesians, 2 Thessalonians, 1 and 2 Timothy, and Titus are pseudonymous works which imitate and often develop Paul's style and thought. These two questions about the relationship between the Acts of the Apostles and Paul's writings, and about the authenticity of the Pauline Corpus will not concern us unduly, but mention of them is fundamental to any comment on Paul's life and work, because the views taken may affect the outcome of the study.

It has been stressed that there were three main influences in St Paul's life and thought, namely: 'the interpenetration of history, theology and ethics'.[26] In other words, Paul was in constant dialogue with events, the specific needs of his readers and his ever-developing theology. In Paul's writing we do not, therefore, find a preconceived theology which is applied in an unchanging way to his ministry. The theology is, rather, emergent in the ministry and the relationship between the two is not always a consistent one. Paul, apparently, allowed himself little time for theological reflection for its own sake. What he always did was to think and respond theologically to the problems and opportunities which his unfolding ministry presented. What, we may ask, motivated Paul in this work? It has been interestingly suggested that he believed his task of proclaiming the gospel to the nations to be an integral part of the things which had to be accomplished before the return of the Lord in glory.[27] If correct, this suggestion throws light on the, otherwise, mysteriously frenetic compulsion which drove him.

However, Paul was more than a proclaimer of the gospel, he was also a remarkable pastor. There are three main evidences of this. First, throughout his writings he shows a concern to help his readers understand the practical implications of the gospel he proclaimed. Often we find a change of key in his narratives which illustrates this. In Romans 12.1ff, for example, he begins to work out the implications of the understanding of the gospel contained in the earlier chapters of the epistle. Second, Paul recognizes that the Christian life is a life in community, hence his repeated emphasis on the importance of belonging to the 'body' of Christ. He did much to help create the early Christian communities and also to help them when they met with dissension and difficulty. Third, Paul showed himself ever ready to minister to individuals and their particular needs. All these are fundamental reasons why the study of his writings is crucial to the study of Christian pastoral theology.

The theological motif which is central to Paul's life and work is that of the 'new righteousness' which is possessed not by striving for it, but by faith (Rom 9.30–10.4). This righteousness is a 'power which not only justifies sinners and restores them to acceptance with Him, it also keeps them in the faith and makes them righteous'.[28] It is important to stress that for Paul, righteousness is a religious rather than an ethical concept. Important, because of the ethical connotations the use of the word now has in common speech. It denotes, for Paul, a new relationship with God, what may be called a 'rightwising' with him.[29] It places the believer in a totally different order of things than previously, it is the opposite of sin and alienation. It is the ground of a new life in Christ, the cause of a 'new creation' (Gal 6.15) in the life of the believer. This was brought about by the free action of God through grace, nothing else. This idea determined all Paul's actions and relations with the churches. 'A different gospel from this, one for example that limited God's freedom and disparaged His grace by insisting on circumcision as a qualification for salvation, was not a gospel at all; it belonged to a different category.'[30]

This insight into the new nature of the human–divine relationship in Christ (1 Cor 5.17) received frequent expression in Paul's writings and it is interesting here to reflect on a similarity of outlook with the Gospel of Matthew. Recall that we saw that the doctrine of rewards in Matthew's Gospel should be seen not as a crude seeking for reward, but as a seeking for an assurance of salvation in the absence of that previously given by the Law. As a rabbinic convert to Christianity, albeit one who very soon moved far from his rabbinic origins, Paul's early formation as a Christian must also have been preoccupied with the same question; how can I know that I am saved? With such a concern it is little wonder that 'justification by faith' becomes a central feature of Paul's theology. This is a 'faith' which accepts what God offers and beyond that requires no human effort. 'So also David pronounces a blessing on the man to whom God reckons righteous apart from works' (Rom 4.6). In other words, righteousness becomes the free gift of God and is the manifestation of his grace in human life (Rom 3.24, 4.4; Gal 2.21). All this leads to a new way of life in Christ (1 Cor 12.31). The power of this life is eternal (Rom 6.23) and entry into it is gained by the future resurrection (1 Cor 15). There is no area of human life and experience, either side of the grave, which remains impervious to the saving power of new life (Rom 8.31–39). No sin, no act of the flesh, no law, or no power can any longer exercise ancient bondage and dominion. With such a powerful and resolute conviction it is little wonder that this theology came to be misconstrued; 'Let us do evil that good may come' (Rom 3.8). The abundance of assurance inevitably led some to suppose that repeated transgression and repentance was the best way to receive repeated salvation. Paul's answer to this was to say that the new freedom created by the faith carried with it obligations which prevented this misunderstanding.

Paul described himself as the servant of Jesus Christ (Rom 1.1) and, in so doing, believed that he was emulating him in the divine work (Phil 2.7ff). Paul, of course, had to produce some credentials for this authority. He did this by recounting his vision of the risen Lord at his conversion. Further to this, Paul cites the record of what Christ had subsequently achieved through him in the Gentile Mission (Rom 15.18). In phrases which echo the call of Jeremiah, Paul (Gal 1.15) claims that time was set aside for this divine work 'before I was born'. Such an emphasis on his own authenticity may well have been prompted by it being questioned, but it goes to show how conscious he was of the presence of the divine purpose in all that he did. Perhaps here we touch on a more profound level of his life and thought. Paul, as we shall see, was an architect in the sense that he laboured to build the sort of Christian communities in which the life of the righteous could be fulfilled. To achieve this he felt that he was justified in the exercise of direct influence over the leaders of such communities. This required immense authority and, perhaps also, manifest levels of coercion as the communities struggled for their existence in an often alien environment where the delay of the second coming of Christ made it the more imperative that they survived indefinitely.

In *The Cost of Authority*, Graham Shaw commenting on the place of power and authority in Paul's ministry writes:

the Pauline prayers, for instance, are not simply an early chapter in the history of Christian spirituality: in their context they have a blatantly manipulative function. The eschatological fantasies of the early believers are constantly exploited to inculcate an anxiety which only membership of the Apostle's privileged community can allay. A rationale of persecution is put forward which makes Paul's position unassailable and provides him with fertile means of projecting his image. Accounts are given of hostility and dissent which enable them to be discounted. Repeatedly in writing to communities which he has founded, the privileges he accords to his readers compel them to assent to his own privileged position.[31]

This comment draws important attention to an aspect of Paul's personality. We are encouraged to see him as one who will stop short of no means of achieving his end, an end which includes the prominence of himself as architect of and pastor to the primitive Christian and especially Gentile Christian communities. As Shaw recognizes, however, this far from vitiates the scope of Paul's achievement.[32] What it does, rather, is give us some insight into the complex social psychology which lay behind it. The picture which emerges is one of a Paul whose personal drive borders on an egotism which reveals the imperfections of his character. The same has been true of many Christians pastors ever since and will yet be of others. With all this in mind we can avoid the over-veneration of Paul and his work, a common danger, and in so doing see that his imperfections, in so many ways, mirror our own. At this point, too, we should keep in mind hermeneutical questions about the limits of our ability to understand, for whatever purpose, the mind of Paul. Try though we may, we must remain largely ignorant of why Paul thought and behaved as he did. In what follows we will examine, from the point of view of pastoral theology, some of the remaining principal features of his ministry and writing.

Paul wrote for individuals and communities who were perplexed about what the new life in Christ required of them. Again and again he returns to this theme, arguing that Christian commitment requires a particular way of life. The Gospels, presuming that the Pauline communities had access to any of them at all, or to the oral traditions which lay behind them, were less than clear on what sort of total life Christians ought to lead. They tended, as we have noted, to raise rather than to answer questions about it. And the longer the second coming was delayed the more imperative these questions became. Paul wrestles with them, for example, throughout the Corinthian correspondence in which he argues that the new life is to be one which imitates Christ. But, as we have seen, there was genuine confusion about what this meant. Conscious of the importance of the question and of the difficulty in answering it, Paul writes (1 Cor 11.1) 'be imitators of me, as I am of Christ'.

It is often observed that this is an example of Paul's egotism and it may well be, but that is not the whole of the story. What, in fact, lies behind this apparent egotism can, rather, be seen to be of profound pastoral significance. Dare we suppose that in the injunction to his Corinthian readers to imitate him, Paul shows that he had discovered the historical importance of the exemplary responsibility of each generation of Christians to the next? It was, we must assume, largely through the influence of Paul in this way that the principle of the imitation of behaviour by example was clearly established. It is interesting to note that in the second century, the exploration of what was meant by the Christian way of life became of central importance. By then, the immediate influence of the early charismatic figures, such as Paul, had passed and the Christianity of Conciliar orthodoxy had not yet been established.

For these reasons Christian orthodoxy was focused on Christian behaviour which had been learned and passed on from generation to generation. Indeed, it was even commented upon that a strong point of the Christian faith was that it enabled untutored people to lead the sort of life they did.[33]

This observation was probably prompted because it was classically supposed by the Greeks that, as virtue was derived only from knowledge, only the learned could be virtuous. The break with this view was, again, arguably one of the achievements of Paul's interpretation of Christianity. In Romans 7.13ff, he argues explicitly that the good is not simply derived from knowledge, because of the way that the perversity of our natures corrupts knowledge. The result of such an insight was that the moral life was seen as a spiritual, rather than as an intellectual, achievement. This insight is central to the Christian view of virtue and can clearly be traced from the Gospels through to the teaching of St Paul where it receives repeated mention. The fact that it became a central part of Christian orthodoxy in the second century must have had a great deal to do with the fact that St Paul gave it such importance in the first.

Reflection on the place of pastoral concern in the ministry of Paul in this way is important, not because we discover answers to pastoral questions which are eternally relevant and binding, but because when we interpret our reading of Paul's writings in the light of our knowledge of their time and our knowledge of Paul's wider purposes and aspirations, we see his remarkably creative theological and pastoral ability at work. That this ability was culture-bound, not always as worked out as it might have been, perhaps even manipulative in some considerable measure and even often mistaken, does not detract at all from its pastoral achievement and the value of the example it sets. It is essential for us to obtain a detailed knowledge of this achievement if we are to discover how Jesus' message of the Kingdom became a gospel about a way of life lived in the midst of the still all too familiar human confusions. This is the making of the biblical faith in action and particularly in its pastoral dimension. It is moreover of great significance to all who would seek to understand Christian pastoral theology and care and the relation of those things to the gospel on the one hand and to human cares and concerns on the other. Nothing was done or advised by Paul unless it was guided by some theological principle which, in particular, means by Paul's theology of righteousness. Paul, as J. T. McNeill observes, quoting M. Schlunk, 'possessed the gift of the care of souls (*seelsorg*) in outstanding measure and employed the art with wonderful mastery'.[34] Paul's vision was of a new life in Christ (1 Cor 5.17) made possible by the decisive act of God in human history (Rom 5.6–11) and which gives rise to 'a still more excellent way' (1 Cor 12.31). In this, on repentance, sinful human beings receive God's grace and with it an assurance of salvation, no matter how great the depravity of their sin. The old orders of human bondage were giving way to a new order based on the Kingdom in a life of reconciliation with God lived out in love.

So far in this chapter, we have been considering ways in which the study of the Bible is essential to Christian pastoral theology and, in doing so, we have seen that this is assisted, rather than prevented, by using every critical means available to us in the study of the biblical texts. Our major discovery is that all of the Bible *is* pastoral theology. Rather, therefore, than concentrate on selected biblical texts and passages for the construction of pastoral theology, we have focused on the pastoral significance of its entirety by looking at the essentially pastoral nature of its central themes. However, the making of pastoral theology does not stop there. The biblical faith, as we have argued throughout, has long been and still is 'in the making'. This is why the study of that history is also a resource for pastoral theology which is equal to, though different from, biblical study. In its turn, of course, the biblical faith as we make it will be studied by others as they strive to do the same thing.

Christian tradition

The ways in which Christian theology has studied the past have been influenced by the different theological presuppositions which are held by those who do it. Roman Catholic scholars, for example, have traditionally understood the past under the magisterial influence of St Thomas Aquinas and through the interpretation of him in innumerable Church documents. In this tradition, the study of the past has been, and in some instances still is, strictly controlled in an authoritative way with the notion of 'authentic interpretation' playing a central role. The Eastern Orthodox Church, on the other hand, appeals only to the first seven Ecumenical Councils. The Reformation in general, and the Lutheran tradition in particular, subjects everything to the principle of *sola scriptura*, that is, to its reading of the biblical text, against which it tests every subsequent development. Anglicanism has been noticeably free, for obvious historical reasons, of attempts to control 'politically' its access to the past. Traditions within Anglicanism have, rather, been profoundly influenced by individual scholars. Such different confessional approaches to the study of the past are, however, now less distinctive than they were. With the possible exception of the approach of Eastern Orthodoxy, it is now often difficult to identify approaches to the past with a particular confession. The main reason for this is the impact which modern historiography has had on scholarship in all the Christian traditions. This has been most keenly felt, as we have seen, in biblical studies, but it applies also to the study of every previous period in Christian history. The rise of disciplines such as the 'philosophy of history', the 'sociology of knowledge', and of 'hermeneutics' have all contributed to the opening of intra-confessional debates about the relevance of the past to contemporary Christian theology. A central problem in all this which will be discussed in the next chapter is that of 'Christianity and culture'. The problem, that is, of how a religion with a specific historical past can become 'inculturated' in any historical present such as our own. This, as we shall see, is a crucial issue for pastoral theology. But before we turn to that, some preliminary considerations about the contemporary study of the past will be necessary.

Philosophies of history attempt to show how various historical methods and presuppositions influence what we can or cannot accept as reliable historical knowledge. They aim to bring a degree of objectivity to bear on the way history is studied, as we have already mentioned in Chapter 1. This aspiration to objectivity is, loosely, challenged by theories about the 'sociology of knowledge'. These theories point out that what can be known at all, the past included, is influenced, in the sense of being constrained by, the social setting in which it is known. The point here is, of course, that ideas and events which occurred in the past are largely obscure to us and may even differ so radically from our own understanding that the two cannot be related. Put another way, this view stresses that in every historical period there are, so to speak, 'glasses' through which everything is seen, and they cannot be taken off. This is why we can never be sure about the extent to which our claims to know anything are limited by our contemporary vision, or lack of it. Theories about the sociology of knowledge attempt to help us with this difficulty. For that reason, they are to be welcomed as we attempt to unravel the sense in which claims to know anything are an inextricable part of the historical and cultural setting in which they occur.

More specifically for our purpose, the study of hermeneutics is of assistance. Indeed, the word 'hermeneutics' itself has become something of a bane to much contemporary philosophical discussion, where it is used perhaps too frequently and without definition. But the study of hermeneutics does present us with at least the possibility of unblocking our inescapably culture-bound knowing, even if only in some small degree. The term comes from Hermes, the messenger of the gods in Greek mythology, who was frequently referred to as 'Interpres', the interpreter. He interpreted the past for the benefit of the present, which is just what the study of hermeneutics, at its best, helps us to do.

Although the modern study of hermeneutics, from its early beginnings in the eighteenth century, was confined mostly to the study of the biblical texts, by the beginning of the nineteenth century it was more generally applied to the study of all historical texts. Earlier in that century, Schleiermacher was largely influential in bringing about this wider application of the notion, and in this he was followed by Dilthey and others. 'Hermeneutics is the art, science or technique, of converting what is not immediately intelligible into a form which is revelatory of meaning.'[35] The presupposition must always be made that the meaning of the past will not always be self-evident to us at all, and that before we can understand it at all disciplined and critical study is always necessary. In such study 'interpretation' is the key element. The problem it raises can be simply put: how do we know, if ever we can, that our interpretation of some past historical text or event is the correct one? And, again, what would we take 'correct' to mean in this context? Interpretation is crucial because forms of expression which were used to convey precise meanings in the past might well not convey those meanings for us and may well, indeed, convey meanings to the contrary.

For this reason, the hermeneutical problem may be stated as follows. To mean the same in the present as a writer might have meant in the past, we may have to say something seemingly quite different, but if we do say something different, how do we know that we mean the same thing as was originally meant? That is the hermeneutical problem. It raises further questions. For example, can we ever know what another author actually meant? Does it, in fact, matter, providing we glean some meaning from what she or he might have written? Do such meanings admit of singular interpretation anyway, or are they much more varied and dynamic? Yet again, are some claims to know what was meant in the past little more than thinly disguised ways of justifying particular views in the present? Reflecting on questions such as these, many writers on hermeneutics have referred to what is known as the 'hermeneutical circle'. This attempts to show that in any active interpretation of meaning the reader is confronted by the text, the text by the reader, and so on, in a continuous circle of dialogue and interpretation. Gadamer, in writing of this circle, points out that it 'describes understanding as the true interplay of the movement of tradition and the movement of the interpreter'.[36]

If for no other reason than that it has recently been neglected, it is important to remember that the study of the past is essential in Christian pastoral theology. Attempts at it have raised questions about the status of written texts in relation to spoken language and about the differences between explanation and interpretation.[37] There are no assured results in this debate. Indeed, the nature of the subject is such that it is difficult to imagine that there ever will be. Another issue concerns the way we select texts for study in the first place. This selection will probably say more about our views and interests than about the significance of the texts in their own period and right. We should, therefore, always try to be clear about why particular texts are chosen for any given purpose. Yet another concerns the way we study texts by interpreting them in the context of what we know, independently, of the life and times in and for which they were written. This is invariably complicated by the fact that, quite often, our knowledge of that context comes only from the texts themselves. It is for reasons such as these that the previously mentioned debate about hermeneutics is so important.

In this process of selecting pastoral texts it will also be necessary to ask what counts as a text in the first place? The answer to this question is not always obvious, for a number of reasons. Pastoral matters are frequently discussed in the context of other issues, such as theological, doctrinal or historical ones. This means that the specifically pastoral material often has to be extrapolated, as far as it is ever possible to do so, from the rest. Further, what counts as a pastoral concern at all changes from period to period. What might appear to be of pastoral importance and significance to one age may not appear to be so to another. For example, post-Reformation discussion about predestination may now appear to us to have been largely doctrinal and philosophical in nature, but in its time it undoubtedly reso-nated with very real practical anxieties which people had about whether or not they were eternally saved. Indeed, preoccupations about eternal salva-tion seem to have been a widespread feature of every previous age but not to the same extent of our own; a fact which, if true, will make it all the more difficult for us to understand not only what they meant, but also and more importantly, how they felt.

In the study of a subject such as pastoral theology it is also necessary for us to compare historical texts with each other, thereby comparing not just some given text with our own understanding, but looking at more than one previous text in an attempt to extrapolate meaning from them generally. In all this the ever-changing dynamics of different times and understandings need to be remembered. Only in the final stages of our attempts to understand the past in this way, will we be able to risk saying anything about its relevance for the present.[38]

Notes

1   Barr, J. (1977) *Fundamentalism*, p. 1. London: SCM.
2   See Nineham, D. H. (1978) *The Use and Abuse of the Bible*, p. 1. London:
     SPCK.
3   See Baumgartner, W. 'The Wisdom Literature', in Rowley, H. H., ed. (1951)
     The Old Testament and Modern Study, pp. 210–37. Oxford: Oxford
     Paperbacks.
4   Von Rad, G. (1962) *Old Testament Theology*, vol. 1, p. 421. Edinburgh:
     Oliver and Boyd.
5   Ibid., p. 425.
6   Israel, Martin (1997) *Doubt: the Way of Growth*, pp. 13–25. London:
     Mowbray.
7   See Perrin, N. (1974) *What is Redaction Criticism?*, London: SPCK.
8   See Tuckett, C. M. (1983) *The Messianic Secret*, Philadelphia: Fortress Press.
9   Cf. Best, E. (1981) *Following Jesus: Discipleship in the Gospel of Mark*,
     Sheffield: JSOT.
10   Conzelmann, L. (1960) *The Theology of St. Luke*, London: Faber & Faber.
11   Cf. Borg, Marcus J. (1994) *Jesus in Contemporary Scholarship*, Pennsylvania:
     Trinity Press, for an excellent contemporary survey.
12   Bultmann, R. (1952) *Theology of the New Testament*, vol. 1, p. 3. London:
     SCM.
13   Ibid., p. 33.
14   Ibid., p. 19.
15   Bornkamm, G. (1960) *Jesus of Nazareth*, p. 26. London: Hodder &
     Stoughton.
16   See Grant, R. (1963) *A Historical Introduction to the New Testament*, pp.
     284–377. London: Collins Fontana Library.
17   Schweitzer, A. (1910) *The Quest of the Historical Jesus*, London: A & C
     Black.
18   Cf. Borg, M. J. (1994) *Jesus in Contemporary Scholarship*, p. 7. Pennsylvania:
     Trinity Press.
19   Crossan, J. D. (1993) *The Historical Jesus: the Life of a Mediterranean Jewish
     Peasant*, p. 417. Edinburgh: T & T Clark.
20   Ibid., pp. 421–2.
21   Elford, R. J. (1982) 'The use of a parable in pastoral care'. *Contact*, 74, 2–6.
22   Abrahams, I. (1917) *Studies in Pharisaism and the Gospels*, p. 55. Cambridge:
     Cambridge University Press.
23   See Sanders, E. P. (1985) *Jesus and Judaism*, pp. 174–209. London: SCM.
24   Dunn, J. D. G. (1998) *The Theology of Paul the Apostle*, p. 2. Edinburgh: T &
     T Clark.
25   Ibid., p. 132.
26   Barrett, C. K. (1985) *Freedom and Obligation*, p. 17. London: SPCK.
27   Munck, J. (1959) *Paul and the Salvation of Mankind*, p. 40. London: SCM.
28   Ziesler, J. A. (1983) *Pauline Christianity*, pp. 96–7. Oxford: Oxford University
     Press.

29 See Sanders, E. P. (1981) *Paul and Palestinian Judaism*, second impression, pp. 502–8. London: SCM.
30 Barrett, *Freedom and Obligation*, p. 54.
31 Shaw, G. (1983) *The Cost of Authority*, pp. 181–2. London: SCM.
32 Ibid., p. 23.
33 See Wiles, M. (1966) *The Christian Fathers*, pp. 160–1. London: Hodder & Stoughton.
34 McNeill, J. T. (1951) *A History of the Cure of Souls*, p. 80. New York: Harper & Row.
35 Boucher, David (1985) *Texts in Context*, p. 20. The Hague: Nijhoff.
36 Gadamer, H. G. (1975) *Truth and Method*, p. 261. London: Sheed & Ward.
37 See Ricoeur, Paul (1974–1975) 'Metaphor and the main problem of hermeneutics'. *New Literary History*, 4, p. 96.
38 McNeill, J. T. (1951) *A History of the Cure of Souls*, New York: Harper & Row, remains an immensely useful introduction to the subject, although its chapters on the Bible are now dated. Its main emphasis is on the cure of souls in the Reformed tradition. Clebsch, W. A. and Jaekle, C. R. (second edition, 1985) *Pastoral Care in Historical Perspective*, Englewood Cliffs, NJ: Prentice-Hall, also remains extremely useful.

Past and present

In the first two chapters we considered the pastoral nature of Christian theology and the difference our religious tradition or view of humanity makes to the understanding of the pastoral. In the third we considered the internal resources found within the Judaeo-Christian tradition which shape pastoral theology. The past, as we have seen, cannot be ignored, but neither can modernity. How do we relate the two? This question is now high on the agenda of pastoral theology. Books by Tom C. Oden, of Drew University in New Jersey, USA have made important contributions to our understanding of the history of pastoral theology and care and their relation to the present. Among them are *Pastoral Theology: Essentials of Ministry* (*PT*) (Harper & Row 1983), and *Care of Souls in the Classic Tradition* (*CT*) (Fortress Press 1984). We will discuss them briefly in turn. *PT* is about ministry in the sense that it considers pastoral theology to be 'that branch of Christian theology which deals with the office and function of the pastor'. I have written elsewhere in some criticism of this view, on the grounds that it limits both the scope of pastoral theology and, at the same time, sharpens the distinction between ministerial and lay pastoral theology and care.[1] The strength of the volume is that it places contemporary theological studies back into the older context of the theological disciplines. 'Pastoral theology is as deeply indebted to historical theology and ecclesiastical history as to systematic teaching and social ethics.'[2] Throughout *PT*, Oden discusses aspects of pastoral work and study in the context of older discussions of the same and, in doing so, he assembles immensely detailed and useful bibliographies. In addition, an extended bibliography is included as an appendix. The care of the poor and the sick and the dying are helpfully discussed in this way. This work may be criticized, however, for emphasizing the tradition at the expense of examining its relationship with modern insights. However, both works stand as illuminating examples of one way in which contemporary pastoral theology and care can be studied in the light of older traditions. They are offered by Oden as a way in which pastoral theology and care can 'recover a lost identity'. As already mentioned, it is, perhaps, a pity that the whole discussion is set in the contemporary context of what ministers (alone) do. *CT* is a volume in the series on theology and pastoral care of which the general editor is Don Browning. In the foreword to the series, Browning writes:

> Our purpose in the theology and pastoral care series is to present ministers and church leaders with a series of readable books that will (i) retrieve the theological and ethical foundations of the Judaeo-Christian tradition of pastoral care (ii) develop lines of communication between pastoral theology and other disciplines of theology; (iii) create an ecumenical dialogue on pastoral care; and (iv) do this in such a way as to affirm yet go beyond the recent preoccupations of pastoral care with secular psychotherapy and the other social sciences.[3]

In *CT* Oden continues his quest for the recovery of the lost identity of Christian pastoral thought and action. He pays particular attention to the *liber regulae pastoralis* of Gregory the Great, bishop of Rome in 590–604. This work is usually translated as *Pastoral Care* after the first two words of the text. According to Oden, Gregory 'articulately gathered up the pastoral wisdom of the patristic period and energetically set in motion the basic direction of the mediaeval pastoral tradition'.[4] Oden claims that it is the most influential book in the history of Christian pastoral tradition. It stresses: the need for an infinite variety of pastoral responses, the need to avoid self-deception by taking Christ's care for us as a model of our own care for others, and the importance of assuming the role of a servant as the only source of pastoral authority. This, in the context of Gregory's theology and spirituality, presents what Oden calls a perennially plausible model for pastoral interpretations. Here, again, we need to exercise some caution and ask whether we can go back to such a tradition as directly as this, particularly when there is so much in that tradition, such, for example, as its attitude towards women, which is now clearly unacceptable. Regardless of issues such as this, Oden argues throughout that what is needed in the present is a deeper and more thorough knowledge of the past. He forcefully repeated this in *After Modernity, What?* in 1992 by arguing that contemporary religious leadership, in general, had persistently withheld its gift to the present of its knowledge of that past and 'instead ... whored after each successive stage of modernity's profligacy'.[5] As an alternative, again, he advocates that Christian theology should recover 'its historical identity, its power to redeem (and) its radical claim to the human spirit. The happy task of theology is to rediscover and reveal the message under the garish modern overlay.'[6] In *Two Worlds* (1992) he applied this consistent theme of his work to the argued death of modernity in America and Russia.[7]

Elsewhere Oden argued that six selected twentieth-century pastoral writers (Hiltner, Clinebell, Oates, Wise, Tournier, and Stollenberg) had lost their contact with classical tradition.[8] Their writings contain no reference to Christian tradition, that is, to the writings of Augustine, Baxter, Calvin, Chrysostom, Cyprian, Gregory, Herbert, Luther, Taylor and Tertullian (as representative examples). By contrast, he found one hundred and fifty four such references in a similar selection of nineteenth-century pastoral writings. Even more notable, he observed, was the fact that the twentieth-century writers abounded with references to Freud, Jung, Rogers, Fromm, Sullivan and Berne (a total of three hundred and thirty). From this evidence, Oden concluded 'contemporary psychotherapists are far more inwardly important and objectively authoritarian for pastoral counselling today than are the writers of the classical tradition of Christian pastoral care'.[9] In an emphasis which ran counter to his own previous writing, Oden called for a major effort 'to re-discover and re-mine the classical models of Christian pastoral care'.[10] Indeed, his own writings have made a valuable contribution to this task which, he notes, importantly, is made all the more urgent because of the now widespread realization that many, if not all, of the modern psychotherapies produce results which are no better than those which occur through spontaneous remission, which occurs in something like 65 to 72 per cent of all cases. The further suspicion that some psychotherapies may even induce injurious dependence on themselves can be added to this. Whilst this rejection of modernity may be considered too harsh, Oden is making an important point. How, then, in the light of such an observation, do we relate tradition to modernity in Christian pastoral theology? This problem is not a new one. It is perennial in the study of the relationship between Christianity and culture and that study is as old as Christianity itself.

Although it initially drew on Jewish thought forms, emergent Christianity soon found it necessary to embrace non-Jewish ones. As the Gentile Mission took Christianity to people for whom Jewish thought forms meant little or nothing, so those forms lost their original meanings. A classical example of this is the way, in the Gentile Mission, that Jesus is referred to less as Messiah (a Jewish title) and more as Lord (a gentile one).[11] As we have briefly seen in the last chapter, it is in the writings of St Paul that we see the early emergence of a distinctively gentile theology. The tension which was implicit in this was one which, inevitably, worked itself out in the life of the early Church as older ways of thinking gave way to newer ones. So much so, that the tension became a major issue by the time of Tertullian (c. 160–220). His famous contempt for all forms of non-Christian learning is expressed in his much quoted question, 'What indeed has Athens to do with Jerusalem; the academy with the church?'[12] Socrates, Tertullian insisted, did not know God in Christ and the *summum bonum* of Plato had nothing to do with God the Father. Tertullian went on to argue that the schisms which had occurred among Christians came from those which were implicit in the secular learning which Christianity had mistakenly embraced and not from the Christian tradition itself. He called for a Christianity expunged of all non-Christian learning and united in its attention only to its own tradition. Such a radical denunciation of external sources did not, however, in the end prevail. Other writers, such as Clement, Origen, and supremely St Augustine, synthesized Christian and non-Christian insight to provide the West with a theology which was at one with the best of non-Christian learning and which was in turn, therefore, not overtly threatened by it. The methods, if not always the conclusions, of thinkers such as these have served as the models of all subsequent mainstream discussion of Christianity and culture in the West.

So the question we are asking about the relationship of modernity to tradition in pastoral theology is far from new. Moreover, it is a question that will never go away this side of the Kingdom of God, as ever-renewing secular knowledge holds promise for the amelioration of the human lot. All this raises the perennial question about the relationship of Christ to culture. Consideration of a classic analysis of this will further our understanding of the relationship of pastoral theology to the past in general and to culture in particular.

In *Christ and Culture*, first published in 1951, H. Richard Niebuhr offered definitions of both terms and, drawing on historical examples, produced a typology of their relation. He leaves the reader, however, to draw her or his own conclusions about the preferability of any of the relations therein defined. Niebuhr defines Christ as one who exists as 'the focusing point in the continuing alternation of movements from God to man and man to God'.[13] This gives Jesus 'power and attraction' which is derived from his Sonship to the Father. We shall later question this definition of Christ. Culture, conversely, is 'the name we give to our artificial secular environment, which man superimposes on the natural'.[14] Following Malinowski, Niebuhr argues that this comprises language, habits, ideas, beliefs, customs, social organization, inherited artefacts, technical processes and values; what New Testament writers might have meant by 'the world'. So understood, culture is a human achievement. It is distinguished from nature by the 'evidences of human purposiveness and effort'.[15] How can Christ and culture, so defined, be related? Niebuhr answers this question by showing how this relationship has, in fact, been understood by influential writers. He categorizes them into five distinctive positions. The first emphasizes opposition between the two concepts. Here a choice is made for Christ against culture. An example is the style used in the Johannine literature of the New Testament where Christ and 'the world' are juxtaposed throughout. Tertullian is cited as an exemplar of this position, in spite of some emphases in his writings which might qualify this interpretation of him. For him, sin originated in human achievement (culture) and the only remedy for it was to bring about an unconditional return to exclusive Christian tradition. Here Niebuhr considers Tertullian to be 'one of the foremost illustrations of the anti-cultural movement to be found in the history of the Church'.[16] Tolstoy is mentioned as a latter-day exemplar of this position.

Diametrically opposed to the first position is that which identifies Christ with culture. Here Christianity is seen, in contrast, as the fulfilment of all cultural hopes and aspirations. The theological hallmark of this position is found in the belief that understands 'the transcendent realm as continuous in time or character with the present life'.[17] Again, Niebuhr gives historically early and late examples of this position. The first is that of Gnosticism, in which Christianity was seen as confirming all that Gnostics believed about the duality of good and evil and of spirit and matter. Rather than challenging Gnostic assumptions, Christianity, so understood, confirmed them. Niebuhr traces this tradition in modern thought from Abelard to Ritschl and considers other examples as diverse as aspects of Roman Catholicism, English Rationalism, the Reformation, and the liberal visionary outlook in general. What this unlikely company, it is argued, frequently have in common is the belief that *their* values, customs and achievements are confirmed by Christ. Another thing they frequently have in common is opposition to nature and this serves to enhance their cultural achievements. Such cultural religion manifests itself in many different ecclesiastical and political ways, all of which symbolize and maintain the closeness of Christ's identification with culture, which they identify as the *status quo*.

Three remaining positions are to be found between these two extremes, and they are distinguished from each other only 'by the manner in which each attempts to combine the two authorities'.[18] In the third position, like the second, Christianity is seen as the fulfilment of cultural aspirations. The difference here is that, unlike the cultural Christianity of the second position, it is held that Christ is also discontinuous with culture. 'Christ enters into life from above with gifts which human aspiration has not envisioned and which human effort cannot attain unless he relates men to a supernatural society and a new value-centre.'[19] Here the emphasis is on the synthesis of a Christ 'from above' with a culture 'from below'. St Thomas Aquinas is quoted as the exemplar of this position. For him, Christ always remains far above culture. The two are never confused or identified, but theology can and does relate them to each other. Niebuhr argues that in the eighteenth century Bishop Butler was a further exemplar of this position, as he 'sought to relate science, philosophy, and revelation, the cultural ethics of rational self-love – so eighteenth century English – and the ethics of Christian conscience of the love of God and the neighbour'.[20]

The fourth way in which Niebuhr sees Christ as being related to culture again accepts their separateness by stressing 'that obedience to God requires obedience to the institutions of society and loyalty to its members as well as obedience to Christ who sits in judgement on that society'.[21] Here is a discipleship of two 'worlds' or 'realms', neither of which can ever be related entirely to the other. Niebuhr cites Luther as an exemplar of this position. Here the emphasis is on paradox, as the two centres of allegiance are acknowledged in spite of the tension created between them by doing so. This, Niebuhr acknowledges, is a solution to the problem which will appeal to all 'political defenders of the separation of church and state, economists who contend for the autonomy of the economic life, philosophers who reject the combination of reason and faith proposed by synthesists and cultural Christians'.[22] If there is a recurrent emphasis amongst those who adopt this solution, it is the way that they subject Christ to culture.

The fifth way in which Niebuhr sees Christ as having been related to culture he calls the 'conversionist solution'. Here, as throughout the typology, certain assumptions are shared with other groups: namely that human nature is sinful, in need of redemption, and not, therefore, to be confused or identified with divinity. 'Here the opposition between Christ and all human institutions and customs is to be recognised.'[23] The difference between this position and the third and fourth is that Christ is not separated from culture by being placed either above or below it, rather Christ is seen as the transformer of culture. Here culture is to be converted, or redeemed, in a process which Niebuhr claims has been recognized (and the implication is that it has been recognized rightly) by Clement of Alexandria and Augustine as well as later, partly, by Aquinas, Luther and Calvin. Niebuhr calls this 'a positive and hopeful attitude towards culture'.[24] Here the fall of humankind is distinguished from the creation and this, importantly, allows for two things. First, it takes sinfulness with a radical seriousness, in the sense that it does not seek to ignore its horror. Second, it is able to maintain a belief in the goodness of creation, thereby preserving a belief in the holiness and righteousness of the God who created it.

With these convictions about creation and fall the conversionists combine a third: a view of history that holds that to God all things are possible in a history that is fundamentally not a course of merely human events but always a dramatic interaction between God and human beings.[25]

Practically, this means that, by grace, sinful humans can face any eventuality, however threatening it may seem to be, with the conviction that it can be overcome. We shall later see that this is no small insight and that it is, moreover, one which is now centrally important to Christian pastoral theology and care. As mentioned, Niebuhr refrains from concluding that any of the foregoing paradigms entirely account for the relation of Christ to culture as though any single one of them were all-sufficient solutions to the problem. Each paradigm makes emphases which cannot be ignored, yet each also contains elements which, if distorted, can only be corrected by other views.

Niebuhr's taxonomy is highly regarded, but it contains a fundamental weakness. It assumes that 'Christ' can be defined separately from culture. In other words, it assumes that 'Christ' and 'culture' can be considered as two separate entities which can be brought back together in a certain way. This I will show to be false. However, Richard Niebuhr's typology has been and is likely to remain immensely influential in thinking about the relationship of Christ to culture. In what follows it is modified rather than rejected.

The problem with Niebuhr's taxonomy is that in separately describing Christ and culture he is presupposing a knowledge of the former which is independent of the latter. He presupposes, that is, that Christ can be known in ways which are independent of the way we know other things. In *The Meaning of Revelation*, Niebuhr acknowledges that there is a difficulty with this and writes: 'we can speak of revelation only in connection with our own history, without affirming or denying its reality in the history of other communities in whose life we cannot penetrate without abandoning ourselves and our community'.[26] He, nevertheless, maintains that the knowledge of God in Christ does contain a disclosure which can be held over and against all that is relative, 'to the limited point of view of historic Christian Faith, a reality discloses itself which invites all the trust and devotion of finite temporal men'.[27]

Two influences in Niebuhr's thought are discernible here. They are those of Troeltsch, from whose *Social Teaching of the Christian Churches* he learnt about the significance of social relativity, and that of Karl Barth from whom he learnt of the givenness of revelation over everything that is human. The attempted reconciliation of these two very different theological emphases is the central theme of Niebuhr's theology. How, then, is he able to maintain that our knowledge of God in Christ is something to which we have an access which is affected, but not obscured, by the socio-cultural context in which it is known? The answer to this, according to Niebuhr, is 'by faith'. It is, he argues, by faith alone that we can achieve a knowledge of God; 'one can speak and think significantly about God only from the point of view of faith in him'.[28] Niebuhr's claim to a knowledge of God in Christ which is independent of all other types of knowing (save perhaps knowing value) is based on a claim to a unique sort of knowledge which is acquired by faith. Much of what follows in the rest of his theology, and in *Christ and Culture* in particular, will stand or fall by this. He also stressed that theology should always be confessional rather than apologetic, suggesting, thereby, that theology should arise out of conviction rather than argument. Personal faith is, therefore, a precondition of theological reflection. Such confessional theology runs, of course, totally counter to the view that theology requires an objective analysis which is only possible if the theologian is not committed *a priori* to the truth of the claims being examined. These contrasting views need to be kept in mind as we turn to a brief evaluation of Niebuhr.

Niebuhr, we also need to notice, claims that there are three distinct movements or activities in the study of theology. First, it is necessary to discuss what has been revealed. From this it is possible to put together what might constitute, on any particular issue, a distinctive Christian point of view. Second, the findings of the first stage have to be defined so that they can become useful. Third, that use has to be applied. Many Christians will, doubtless, have little difficulty in accepting Niebuhr's account of our knowledge of God in Christ and with that of accepting also the solution to the Christ and culture problem tentatively implied in his argument. What do we make of his typology, however, if we are not as confident as this about the claim that we can have a knowledge of God in Christ by a faith which constitutes a knowledge which is independent of other forms of knowing?

Indeed, it may be argued that we have never had, nor can ever have, the sort of knowledge of God in Christ which Niebuhr presupposes, simply because the Christ from whom that knowledge is derived is already a cultural interpretation of the historical Jesus, who was apparently, in so many ways, an ordinary person. The gospel writers often record that because of this, he was frequently mistaken for others and, as we have seen, there is an implication in Mark's Gospel that its readers were concerned to know why many who actually met him did not recognize his messiahship. These, albeit shadowy, insights into the ordinary nature of Jesus' person contrast markedly with the popularly held view of him found in the more mainstream interpretation of his person and work. In all this we can trace a process in which the probably very ordinary historical Jesus becomes a highly cultural and stylized figure, as pre-existent cultural concepts and motifs come to be applied to him in the process of attempts to explain who he was. The title 'Messiah' is the earliest example of this, but there are many others.[29]

Such an inculturated Jesus has existed in the popular mind ever since, and always will, notwithstanding the quite proper quests for the historical Jesus which as we have seen have preoccupied so much twentieth-century New Testament scholarship. The fact remains, however, that when we study the Christ of the New Testament, we are in fact comparing the many cultural interpretations of that Christ with our cultural interpretations, rather than comparing an acultural Christ of the New Testament with our culture as Niebuhr suggests. When the study of the person of Christ is undertaken with this in mind, then it is more properly understood as an ongoing cultural dialogue and not, as Niebuhr claims, a dialogue between an historical given on the one hand and culture on the other.

We may, however, still prefer a solution to the problem which is not totally dissimilar from that of Niebuhr, even though we might not accept his theological presuppositions about the nature of our knowledge of God in Christ. Therefore, we may not want to separate Christ from culture, nor identify the two. Nor may we wish to set tradition always over the present or make the present always subject to it. Rather, we may choose to argue that our knowledge of Christ in the tradition, however inculturated it is, does become the means whereby we attempt to transform our present values and experiences. That is not to say that our knowledge of the past will always transform our present attitudes and experiences, only that it may do so. Not to place the present entirely under the judgement of the past in this way, keeps open the possibility that present and future experiences may, in fact, have a transforming effect on our knowledge of the past. For those who suppose that there is in Christianity a once-for-all givenness which settles all pastoral and other questions indefinitely, this modified view of Niebuhr's typology will obviously be unattractive. For others, however, it might show how such an important attempt to understand Christ and culture remains helpful, even if some of its presuppositions are, as we have seen, perhaps not acceptable without qualification. What this attenuated form of Niebuhr's typology enables us to do is to accept the fact that the figure of Christ remains shadowy and often creates uncertainty where so often certainty is desperately sought, particularly, for example, in pastoral and ethical debate.

In Chapters 5 and 6 we will consider, in some detail, the implications of this debate for the study of pastoral theology in both its individual and social settings respectively. Before we do that, however, it will first be helpful to explore, by way of illustration, examples of theological themes which often feature in discussion about tradition and modernity in pastoral theology. The reason for selecting these particular themes will be given, and the discussions are intended to serve only as illustrations of the ways in which contemporary pastoral theology is enriched by the study of Christian tradition. The aspects of pastoral theology we will discuss are anger, grace, sin and peace.

Anger

Anger is such a fundamental element of human experience that no individual ever escapes it. Coming to terms with it is always traumatic, as can be observed in the often prolonged tantrums of young children, as they experience the sheer power of their nascent capacity for anger. It often has a frighteningly destructive power. This can either be directed towards others, in the form of aggression and hostility, or directed inwards in the form of bitterness and resentment which are often associated with guilt and depression. The inward direction of anger, in this way, can be unbelievably personally debilitating. Little wonder then that anger is so frequently associated with darkness and Promethean power. All this illustrates just some of the reasons why anger has proved so difficult to reconcile with love in general and with the love of God in particular. What possible loving purpose can be served by anger? Or does anger destroy love entirely?

In a major study of anger, Alastair Campbell notes that two twentieth-century writers, C. H. Dodd and A. Hanson, both conclude that the relationship between God's love and God's rage and jealousy was to be regarded not as an irreconcilable split in his nature, but as a necessary antinomy.[30] Dodd observes that the wrath of God is 'being revealed against all the impiety and wickedness of those who hinder the Truth by their wickedness'.[31] And Hanson argues that the 'biblical concept of the wrath of God . . . has its place in Christian thought today'.[32]

According to the views of both these writers, which Campbell rejects, anger as a passion could not be thought to be part of the experience of a God of love. At best therefore, all that can be said is that, for some unknown reason, God permits anger. Campbell rejects these ways of reconciling God's anger with his love. At their worst they can inculcate what he calls a gospel of 'chronic niceness' which bears little correlation to the human experience of anger as described briefly above. Such a gospel is inevitably a remote one which has little and in all probability no resonance with the realities of human experience. A reassessment of the nature of anger in psychological study lies behind this theological re-evaluation. Anger is now less often seen as something 'caused' in the sense that the angry person is a helpless cipher of external influences. It is, rather, being studied from a point of view which regards an emotion such as anger more as conduct than reaction.[33] One result of this is that anger can now be construed as a form of conduct which can be active, purposive and even strategic. This clearly runs counter to any belief that individuals cannot ever be held to be responsible for their emotions since, on this view, they can be subject to purposive control. As such, anger is seen as 'the author of its own provocation'.[34] It is purposeful, directed and invariably instrumental. So understood, it has creative as well as destructive powers and should be less feared and more understood for that reason.

Campbell takes a similar view when he argues that anger is a necessary element in the force of love. He gives two reasons for thinking this and they are both explicitly pastoral in nature. First, if humans deny that anger is an integral and instrumental part of God's love, then they alienate themselves and their own experience from that of God. And second, to fail to be angry in the face of great injustice is often also a failure to love. So understood, anger comes to be seen as a sign of hope, a signal that things ought to be changed, and an expression of the conviction that they can be. Campbell points out that if we can understand anger in this way, as an instrument of love, then 'coming to terms with the anger of God (and with our anger at God) may not be so very different from our experience of learning to live in close proximity with our fellow human beings'.[35]

The areas of pastoral thought and practice where what may be called 'instrumental anger' has been particularly prominent are in liberation and feminist theologies. These begin on a note of angry protest against the *status quo*. They refuse to accept that the way things are is the way they ought to remain and, when this is resisted as so often it is, anger is strategically used as a form of reply. It is, as such, often skilfully managed as it pushes resolutely for desired change. The 'just revolution' as an expression of anger is an example of how this is attempted in a combination of emotion and rationality. Here redemption is sought not by turning away from radical evils and injustice, but by tackling them in their own terms, and by angry protest, if necessary. All this, of course, raises ethical problems and we shall consider these in Chapter 6.

For our purpose, it is important to notice that what Campbell has done in this debate is not, simply, to discuss anger only in the terms of contemporary psychology. Rather, while taking note of this, he has also brought the insights of Christian tradition and theology to bear. Whether or not the understanding of anger in Christian tradition can transform secular understandings of it, or simply join with them in creating new insights, remains an open question. But there is clearly a sense here in which the Christian tradition can be seen to be throwing new light on the role of angry protest in human affairs. At the very least, it encourages those responsible for those affairs to give some attention to the Christian tradition.

Conclusive evidence for the transformation of culture by Christ or Christianity along the lines Niebuhr suggests will always, of course, be ambiguous. Complex human affairs are invariably too obscure to allow this. All we can perhaps hope for is that an ongoing dialogue takes place within which some hope for or evidence of transformation will be discerned. In this example, it has been shown that it is helpful to go back to a much more traditional and biblical understanding of the place of God's wrath in the exercise of his righteousness as we try to understand the relationship between anger and justice in the modern world. This well illustrates the sort of possibilities which open up once tradition and modernity are held in a creative and even transforming tension.

Grace

Disagreement over the nature of grace has been recurrent in Western Christianity. Following St Paul, St Augustine took the view that humans do not possess the complete freedom which would be necessary for them to achieve their most desired ends. This is because of *hubris*; a mistaken human belief in self-sufficiency, in which *eros* (human love) becomes self-deluding in thinking it can reach beyond itself. It is only the free action of God's love, *agape*, which can release *eros* from its *hubris* to create a new synthesis in *caritas* (the God-created joining of human and divine love). An external divine action, that is, which releases human love and endeavour from its own inescapable limitations. Such an act of God is what is meant by an act of grace.[36]

Pelagius, by contrast, whilst not denying that God *could* exercise his grace towards humankind, asserted that humans did have the freedom to achieve their most desired ends. God's grace on this view has more of an educative and co-operative relationship with human endeavour, rather than serving simply to displace it. The history of this debate is well known. Here we will only consider some features of its twentieth-century form and note their significance for understanding the relationship of tradition to modernity in pastoral theology.

Christian theologians in the twentieth century have differed from those of the Reformation by seeing grace as an agency in social, political and historical destiny, rather than simply as an act of forgiveness by God in Christ towards the individual sinner. This stems, in part, from the increasing secularization of modern life, in the sense in which that life now asserts its autonomy from divine and ultimately from ecclesiastical control. So understood, secularization is a process with origins reaching back into the dissolution of the mediaeval synthesis between reason and religion and the manifestation of that in a politically unified Christendom. Secularization, so understood, is a process which has visible consequences. Among them is a widespread belief in human self-sufficiency. This leaves no conceptual room for grace, as formerly defined. The problem is that many of the moral problems which now confront us do so because of the successes of our own inventiveness. They have been created, for example, by the success of our technologies in areas such as economics, nuclear sciences, embryology, *in vitro* fertilization and the life-sciences generally. All these activities are of our own making and they bear the marks of our own nature; namely its capacity for good and evil, just as any other human artefact inevitably does. How are we, then, to promote the good which our technologies are capable of and suppress the evil of which they are equally capable? We are, for practical purposes, virtually unable to answer this question, beyond being able to point to some important, but barely adequate, attempts to set up social controls many of which (such as those in embryology) are still of a largely voluntary nature, albeit often self-governed by well-disciplined professions. The theological difficulty here arises from the fact that we are relying on our nature to control the use of the things it has produced. To control, that is, expressions of itself. Can it realistically do this? Does it have the necessary resources? Or does human nature still need to be complemented by divine grace to save it from the misuse of its own inventiveness? Theologians such as Barth, Bonhoeffer, Tillich and Reinhold Niebuhr have all, in their own ways, sought to reply to this question. They have done so, not by denying that there are profound senses in which humans are expected to draw on their own resources, but (a) by attempting to show the limits they meet when they do this, and (b) by showing the real benefits of understanding these limits when they are met by an understanding of divine grace. They have argued, therefore, that human well-being cannot be secured solely through human endeavour. Mention of Reinhold Niebuhr's understanding of grace will illustrate just one way in which this has been done.

Niebuhr's early writings were more concerned with the nature of human sin than they were with God's grace. His attention to the latter is to be found in his occasional writings on specific subjects (over a thousand of them) and in the second volume of his Gifford Lectures *The Nature and Destiny of Man.*[37] Here, as elsewhere, he stresses that liberal Christians and secularists alike have disregarded the doctrine of grace because they have not been prepared to face the truth about the extent of human sinfulness. Niebuhr identifies grace with truth; arguing that the sinful self does not have access to truth, nor does that self possess the freedom of will to obey it even if it has the ability to recognize truth in the first place. That freedom, he argues, can only be granted by Christ, who alone has power to enable sinful humans, both individually and socially, to be freed from their self-limitation. The incarnation and the atonement are the theological concepts through which Niebuhr worked out how grace bears on human affairs. In doing so, he stressed that as well as living the truth of God, Christ was also the power of

God. This power is both over and in the affairs of humankind. Such power is expressed in the form of divine mercy:

> It is possible to appropriate this mercy only through the Christ, whose sufferings disclosed the wrath of God against sin, and whose perfection as man is accepted as normative for the believer, by the same faith which sees in Him, particularly His cross, the revelation of the mystery of the divine mercy triumphing over, without annulling the divine wrath.[38]

This point is crucial to Niebuhr's doctrine of grace. He did not think that divine grace could bring about the complete perfectibility of human nature, because the pretence of that perfectibility was the source of human arrogance in all its forms. The source, too, of the ultimate arrogance and sin; spiritual pride. He identified religion as the vehicle for this and described it, as we shall see below, as 'the last battleground of the human soul before God'. All this for Niebuhr was the 'paradox of grace', in the sense that the very thing that saved humans from their egotism was, at the same time, so often the cause of it. In spite of this, he held to the belief in the also divinely ordained human capacity to receive grace yet avoid egotism:

> If it be true . . . that no sinful self-centredness could ever destroy the structure of freedom and self-transcendence in man, it must follow that there is some inner testimony from the very character and structure of the human psyche against the strategy of sinful egotism.[39]

Niebuhr also claims that the fullness of grace will not occur until the second coming of Christ. The historical present is an interim period in which the mercies of divine grace are but dimly perceived. But he does stress, however, that because of the goodness of creation, there is a continuity between the operation of grace in this world and the next.

These brief remarks give only a slender indication of the profundity of Niebuhr's writing on divine grace. What should be clear, however, is the fact that pastoral theology requires some such thoroughgoing analysis of the human condition, or, more to the point, an analysis of possible remedies for it. Indeed, as mentioned above, the extent to which human autonomy is now established makes it all the more urgent to rediscover ways in which that autonomy can be used to good effect and not become the means of its own destruction. The Christian understanding of grace, as explored by Niebuhr and others, has a profound contribution to make towards this. Here, again, we have considered an example of how the Christian dialogue between tradition and modernity relates to contemporary pastoral concern by showing how a Christian understanding of grace might apply to the present by throwing light on the way in which seemingly unlimited human powers can be directed for the good. In such a way, pastoral theology makes a contribution to striking a balance between recognizing the place for proper human autonomy on the one hand and the need for it to be complemented by divine grace on the other.

Sin

Brief mention has already been made of sin in the foregoing discussion about the relationship of sin to grace in the thought of Reinhold Niebuhr. We will now consider, a little further, something of the contemporary significance of the understanding of sin for pastoral theology, as yet another example of the way in which it provides the means of creating a dialogue between tradition and modernity.

Traditionally, discussions of sin have centred on the sin of Adam and its influence on the subsequent and inherent sin of all human beings. In Western Christianity, the Catholic tradition has held that individual acts of sin must be confessed, since they cut the sinner off from the prevenient grace of God. Protestantism, by contrast, has put less emphasis on sin*s* and more on the state of sin in which all humans, by dint of their humanity, are estranged from God. In both traditions, sin is seen as a profoundly religious concept, and the cause of the alienation of human beings from God. This is an alienation which, in its turn, is the cause of human disorientation and suffering. In all this there is a profundity which modern attitudes to sin often distort. What they invariably share is a rejection of the religious view of the nature of sin and hold, rather, that sin is purely a moral concept.

From the point of view of pastoral theology this should be seen as a trivialization of sin. Who, for example, is to decide if any particular moral transgression constitutes sin? Indeed, in societies which are progressively liberal in outlook and practice, the marginalization and trivialization of sin into nothing but a moral concept has been a seeming inevitability. In such societies, talk of sin has been seen as a barrier to the 'healthy' liberalization of areas of human thought and practice; many of which are, invariably, sexual ones. Furthermore, the understanding of sin as a moral concept and not a religious one has resulted in its relativization. It has been thought to relate only to contingent moral issues and, therefore, to have nothing to do with ultimate values. All of this has been part of a wider human assertiveness which has behaved as though it alone is competent to decide what is sinful and what is not.

More widely, the understanding of sin as a moral concept has severed it from any frame of reference from which it can derive ultimate authority. Traditionally that authority was over the individual through the threat of eternal salvation or damnation. The natural anxiety this caused was exploited by generations of revivalist preachers and still is by some. Even, however, if there is an unacceptable crudity about this, it at least makes the important point that sin has something to do with ultimate human wellbeing. A reminder, that is, that an awareness of sin and a desire to do something about it marks a deep longing in the soul for God.

Finally, understanding sin as a moral concept alone has been associated with the belief that sins are committed exclusively by individuals. This has obscured the fact that sin has as much to do with corporate as it does with individual human doings. Whole societies commit sins and these are often less than obvious because they are disguised as the norm and protected by the *status quo*. Economic sins are common examples of this, especially whenever the poor and weak are deliberately, even if subtly, exploited in order to maintain the material advantage of the rich and powerful. Now more than perhaps ever before, we are beginning to recognize the commonality of the human lot, particularly on a worldwide scale. This forces us to think about human welfare in ways which transcend particular religious or secular outlooks and barriers. At the very least, it is being widely recognized that it is no longer possible to seek security only within the bounds of narrow and exclusive nationalisms. Traditional ideologies which have supported these and gone on to aspire to world domination are having to be rethought, as they come to be seen as the dangerous and unrealizable fantasies that they are and always have been. Christianity, like every other view of life, has to come to terms with finding its place among other religions and ideologies of the world. To quote Reinhold Niebuhr again, 'The ultimate sin is the religious sin of making the self-deification implied in moral pride explicit. This is done when our partial standards and relative attainments are explicitly related to the unconditioned good, and claim divine sanction.'[40] He goes on to stress that because of this,

religion is not simply, as is generally supposed, an inherently virtuous human quest for God. It is merely the final battleground between God and man's self-esteem. In that battle even the most pious practices may be instruments of human pride.[41]

In the quest for anything like a total human understanding which would be sufficient to secure world peace, those who begin from a religious viewpoint have to atone for its inherent pride before they can even begin to bring the insights of their own religion to bear more widely on the common good. A Christian pastoral theology which is at all credible must be mindful of this whenever it seeks, as always it must, to address itself to the human condition and especially to its darker, what the Christian tradition recognizes as its sinful, side.

Peace

The pursuit of peace in the nuclear age has become a central concern for pastoral theology. This will be examined in Chapter 6 where it will be seen that it is an inevitable consequence of a pastoral concern for total human welfare. Here we will consider the bearing of Christian tradition on the contemporary pursuit of peace. The desire for peace is universal. Few have ever glorified war for long and in the twentieth century we know too much about its horror to seek anything but alternatives to it. As the Anglican Bishops at their Lambeth Conferences have repeatedly stated, 'war as a means of settling international disputes is incompatible with the teaching of Jesus'. Such a view, however, does not take us very far unless we deduce from it, as many do, that it enjoins pacifism. Short of this, what is required is some framework within which violence can be controlled and, hopefully, eliminated.

Christian pastoral engagement in the pursuit of peace arises out of fundamental convictions which are to be found deep in Christian tradition. Reflection on this must begin with the study of peace in the biblical traditions. In the Old Testament we find, again and again, that there is a pragmatic acceptance of war as an inescapable fact of life and even an instrument of Yahweh's will. The Song of Moses (Exod 15.1ff) is thought to be one of the oldest pieces of Israelite oral tradition in the Old Testament:

'I will sing to the Lord, for he has triumphed gloriously;
    horse and rider he has thrown into the sea.

> The Lord is my strength and my might,
>> and has become my salvation;
> this is my God, and I will praise him,
>> my father's God, and I will exalt him.
> The Lord is a warrior;
>> the Lord is his name.

Here the Lord's military exploits were seen as the means whereby he accomplished his righteous purposes. Similarly, in the vision of Amos, Yahweh is working out his righteousness not only through the destiny of Israel, but equally through the destiny of the surrounding nations. 'Therefore, thus says the Lord God: "An adversary shall surround the land, and strip you of your defence; and your strongholds shall be plundered"' (Amos 3.11). And again, when the Southern kingdom was about to fall to the armies of Babylon, Jeremiah saw those armies as instruments of the righteous wrath of Yahweh. Such a closeness with the fact of war and its place in Yahweh's purposes, was subsequently tempered in the Old Testament by the expectation of a messianic future in which all war would cease. In Isaiah's song of thanksgiving (Isa 11.6–9), there is a vision of peace which will eliminate all hostilities and ancient enmities and in which 'the earth shall be full of the knowledge of the Lord, as the waters cover the sea'. In the vision of Micah (Mic 4.1ff), the simple picture of people sitting under their own vines and not being afraid, graphically depicts a future when 'nation shall not lift up sword against nation, neither shall they learn war any more'.

The understanding of peace in the New Testament is bound up with the person and work of Jesus. As a proclaimer of the messianic Kingdom (Mark 1.15), Jesus inaugurated a new relationship with God, a new righteousness (Matt 5.20). Participation in this new righteousness meant participation also in the long promised messianic peace (Matt 5.9). For this reason, peacemaking became a present spiritual obligation rather than only a future longing (1 Pet 3.11). Such peacemaking is, therefore, an indispensable element of Christian discipleship. It is what is required of those who follow a Christ whose work was seen as the work of peace (Eph 2.14), 'For he is our peace'. Jesus' ministry was a ministry of peace (Eph 6.14–15), a message which came from God (John 14.27). John is clear about the importance of Jesus' gift of peace to his disciples. When Jesus appeared to his disciples (John 20.19), the first thing he says to them is 'Peace be with you'. Peace is thus seen as a manifestation of the power of God and an important work of the spirit. As a spiritual gift, the gift of peace was an inner experience which first worked itself out in the personal lives of the believers (Acts 4.32–5.11) and in turn in their wider doings. Not much is said about the latter in the New Testament, because of the enforced sectarian nature of early Christianity. Christians did not engage, as such, in wider affairs of state. All that was to come much later after the conversion of Constantine in the fourth century. It is debated whether early Christianity was exclusively pacifist or not and the question is difficult to answer. Undoubtedly, some saw, as they have always seen, that the renunciation of all violence was a necessary condition of Christian discipleship. Others have sought to respect this, but not in a way which prohibits the use of limited violence if it is required by justice. Here we meet the classic tension in the Christian understanding of peace. As a religion of the messianic present, Christianity is clearly required to fulfil that peace. As a religion which yet expects the Messiah to return in glory, Christianity also teaches that the present peace is, and can only remain, imperfect in relation to that which is to come. For probably the majority of Christians this imperfection not only allows, it also requires, the exercise of just and controlled war fighting in the face of unacceptable aggression.

In the fourth and fifth centuries, after Christianity had become the official religion of the Roman Empire, writers such as Ambrose of Milan and St Augustine began to formulate the conditions under which they believed Christians could legitimately engage in war. In doing this, they drew on older approaches to the justice of war found in Greek and, particularly, Roman writings. In this they began a debate which still continues in the Christian tradition. It can be traced back through all the creative periods in the development of Western theology and especially in the writings of St Thomas Aquinas and the Protestant Reformers. The unfolding tradition has distinguished between (a) the conditions which must be fulfilled before war can be begun (*Ius ad Bellum*) and (b) the conditions which have to be observed once it has been (*Ius in Bello*). In outline, these conditions are as follows. War must be declared by a lawfully constituted authority. Its cause must be identified and seen to be just. Resort to war must be a last resort. The harm incurred must be proportionate to the end sought. Ideally, this must cause less harm than would otherwise occur if force had not been used. There must be a reasonable chance of success. In other words, it is not morally justified to begin a war which will end in a defeat and change nothing. These conditions stress, in particular, that war must be fought with the right intention; namely that of establishing peace. From all this two conditions arise. The immunity of non-combatants must be respected by the use of *discriminatory* means and those means must be *proportionate* to the end desired.

In considering the applicability to the present of this ancient discussion about the justice, or otherwise, of war, we meet a good example of the central theme of this chapter: the relationship of tradition to modernity in Christian pastoral thought and practice. Some argue that the tradition has no relevance to the modern world on the grounds that its formulae were created in military and social conditions which were radically unlike those of the present. The existence and deployment of nuclear weapons is sometimes cited as an example of the radically different circumstances which now prevail. This view is mistaken. The formulae of the Just War are as applicable to questions of modern nuclear warfare as they ever have been. That is not to say, of course, that formulae may not have to develop as they have done in the past. But if this happens it will do so as a result of the sustained endeavour to apply the Just War tradition to our own circumstances. Can nuclear weapons be used in accordance with the requirements of the justice of war? Before that question can be answered it will be necessary, briefly, to consider the nature of nuclear weapons.

Non-nuclear (conventional) weapons kill because they create blast and heat. Nuclear weapons also do this, with one exception, but in addition they also kill from the radiation which is generated by their use. The exception is neutron bombs, or enhanced radiation weapons, which do not create blast and heat and kill only as a result of radiation. The harmful effects of such radiation on human beings and the environment is still only partially understood since, with the tragic and partial exceptions of Hiroshima, Nagasaki and Chernobyl, we have no actual experience of radiation occurring suddenly and on an extended geographical scale. We do know, however, that the effects of radiation can be divided into three phases. The initial phase lasts for some twenty-four hours and occurs in a circle around the point of explosion. The intermediate phase occurs when prevailing weather conditions carry irradiated dust away from the explosion, creating the familiar cigar shaped effect. This lasts for some eight to ten days. The final phase of radiation is the so-called residual phase in which irradiated material is blown into the upper atmosphere, remaining there for an indefinite period, from where it gradually returns to earth in normal atmospheric processes. Such residual radiation will cause deaths indefinitely. There is also much debate about whether this phase of radiation would seriously disrupt the earth's atmosphere giving rise to a 'nuclear winter' in which the sun's ultra-violet rays would be prevented from sustaining life over large parts of the earth's surface.

It is unquestionably clear that nuclear war conducted on a substantial scale could not possibly meet the requirements of the Just War tradition. It would be indiscriminate in the sense that it would cause the deaths of innocent civilians, and it would be disproportionate in the sense that no conceivable end could justify death and destruction on such a scale. For many this settles all questions concerning the morality of the use of nuclear weapons and they, therefore, oppose not only their use, but also their deployment as deterrents. There is disagreement about what follows from such a conclusion. Some unilateralists favour the total renunciation and abolition of nuclear weapons by one side unconditionally and immediately. Others proceed more cautiously and believe that the nuclear edifice should be dismantled over a period, by negotiation if possible, notwithstanding the intention to become nuclear free in as short a time as possible. This debate is complicated by the fact that nuclear weapons are formally owned and deployed by some countries and in addition there are a number of countries who either already possess nuclear weapons, or have the ability to do so at a speed which makes their non-possession in the present only technical. Other nations are also thought to be capable of acquiring nuclear weapons at short notice if they wish to do so. The overt possessors of nuclear weapons all claim that they deploy them for peaceful purposes only, and they further claim that without them the peace which does exist would not do so.

For this reason, the debate about the morality of possessing nuclear weapons now focuses on the morality or otherwise of nuclear deterrence theory, since there are few who believe that their use, on any scale, could be morally justified. The difficulty with this arises from the fact that nuclear weapons do not work as deterrents unless the intention to use them, if necessary, is made abundantly clear. It would be impossible to bluff this intention if deterrence failed. The guarantee not to use nuclear weapons, which such a bluff would require if it were to be morally acceptable, is one which cannot, in the nature of the case, be given. This is because their deployment relies on complex social arrangements comprising layers of hierarchical command. Although these are all designed not to fail, that could not be guaranteed and the possibility of a nuclear war occurring by default of the bluff would be a real one. Nuclear deterrence theories are further complicated by the fact that most nuclear possessors claim that, in order to maintain the effectiveness of their systems, they constantly have to be tested and updated. This is one cause of the nuclear arms race. Further considerations caution against the too easy acceptance of nuclear weapons as deterrents. First, their deployment may well help to bring about the conditions of unrest, suspicion and even hatred that it is ostensibly meant to prevent. Second, it contributes to the so-called 'horizontal proliferation' of nuclear weapons as aspiring possessors seek to avail themselves of the peace which nuclear weapons, when deployed as deterrents, ostensibly makes possible. Third, nuclear deterrence may well not be as indefinitely stable as its advocates often suggest. Much hinges on the question of whether nuclear weapons are different in kind from conventional ones. Those who argue they are and that their deployment as deterrents is not morally acceptable thereby, of course, prohibit possession of all nuclear weapons. Others, however, counter this by saying that some small nuclear weapons might have uses which are morally licit in instances where the use of large conventional weapons would not be.

Yet further, the question remains about what to do about the deployment of nuclear weapons, even if the moral arguments against their deployment as deterrents, as well as use, are convincing. Contrary to what is often believed, it does not necessarily follow from the moral prohibition that they should all be disposed of forthwith. The reasons for this will be discussed more fully in Chapter 7 and they relate to the fact that additional considerations have to be made whenever moral judgements are applied to complex social and political situations.

That this is a significant pastoral debate is obvious, since claims to pastoral integrity which ignored the possibility of untold millions of people perishing would have a disturbingly hollow ring. As we have seen, the debate refers to the Bible and Christian tradition in an illuminating way.

The foregoing examples of ways in which contemporary pastoral concern draws deeply on the Bible and Christian tradition have been chosen because they illustrate the way in which it is necessary to maintain a dialogue between tradition and modernity in pastoral debate. What always needs to be sought in this, is a right relationship of the Christ of the Bible and Christian tradition with modernity. When it is achieved, such as it arguably is in the ways we have illustrated, it brings to contemporary pastoral theology and care a beneficial dialogue with tradition which throws light on the present.

Notes

1   Elford, R. J. (1985) 'Pastoral Theology by T. C. Oden', *Contact*, 86, 25–7.
2   Oden, T. C. (1983) *Pastoral Theology: Essentials of Ministry*, p. xi. New York: Harper & Row.
3   Oden, T. C. (1984) *Care of Souls in the Classic Tradition*, p. 7. Philadelphia: Fortress.
4   Ibid., p. 12.
5   Oden, T. C. (1992) *After Modernity, What?*, p. 31. Grand Rapids, Michigan: Zondervan.
6   Ibid., p. 201.
7   Oden, T. C. (1992) *Two Worlds*, Downes Grove, Illinois: IVP.
8   Oden, T. C. (March 1980) 'Recovering lost identity'. *The Journal of Pastoral Care*, vol. XXXIV, no. 1, 4–19.
9   Ibid., p. 12.
10 Ibid., p. 8.
11 See Cullman, Oscar (1959) *The Christology of the New Testament*, pp. 195–237. London: SCM.
12 Tertullian, *On Prescription Against Heretics*, ch. VII, in Roberts, A. and Donaldson, J., eds, *Ante-Nicene Fathers*, vol. 3. Edinburgh: T&T Clark.
13 Niebuhr, H. R. (1975) *Christ and Culture*, p. 29. New York: Harper Colophon.
14 Ibid., p. 32.
15 Ibid., p. 33.
16 Ibid., p. 55.
17 Ibid., p. 84.
18 Ibid., pp. 41–2.
19 Ibid., p. 42.
20 Ibid., p. 140.
21 Ibid., p. 42.
22 Ibid., p. 184.
23 Ibid., p. 43.
24 Ibid., p. 191.
25 Ibid., p. 194.
26 Niebuhr, H. R. (1960) *The Meaning of Revelation*, p. 60. London: Macmillan Paperback.
27 Ibid., p. 16.
28 Ibid.
29 See Cullman, O. (1959) *The Christology of the New Testament*, London: SCM.
30 Campbell, A. V. (1986) *The Gospel of Anger*, p. 6. London: SPCK.
31 Dodd, C. H. (1932) *The Epistle of Paul to the Romans*, p. 24. London: Hodder & Stoughton.
32 Hanson, A. T. (1957) *The Wrath of the Lamb*, p. 198. London: SPCK.
33 See Warner, C. Terry 'Anger and similar delusions', in Harre, R., ed. (1986) *The Social Construction of Emotions*, pp. 135–66. Oxford: Blackwell.

34 Ibid., p. 164.
35 Campbell, *The Gospel of Anger*, p. 92.
36 See Nygren, A. (1953) *Agape and Eros*, p. 474. London: SPCK.
37 Neibuhr, Reinhold (1941) *The Nature and Destiny of Man*, vols 1 & 2. London: Nisbet.
38 Ibid., vol. 2, p. 108.
39 Ibid., vol. 2, p. 121.
40 Niebuhr, R. *The Nature and Destiny of Man*, vol. 1, p. 213.
41 Ibid.

5

Individual care

In the last chapter we asked the question, how do we bring Christian tradition to bear in the modern world? In answer we favoured the view that it should have a 'transforming' relationship which is receptive to the insights of both tradition and modernity alike. I suggested the model of 'Christ in conversation with culture'. We will now consider how, in practice, this might be achieved in the care of individuals. Whilst there is, of course, much about the care of individuals in the Bible and Christian tradition, the twentieth century has seen the considerable development of secular views of the same. Clearly, this is an area where the 'conversation' solution to the relationship between the two can, so to speak, be put to the test.

The study and practice of the care of individuals has been prominent in the Protestant tradition, so much so that this is the traditional domain of pastoral theology. However, the concept of the individual has a history. It derives from the attention the Reformers gave to the notion of individual salvation. This emphasis on individualism was not, however, an invention of the Reformation. It had been emerging in philosophy since at least the time of William of Occam (d. 1349), and was a marked feature of the Renaissance, particularly in the writings of Erasmus for whom individual perception was considered to be the source of truth. The Reformers brought to all this the insights of their theological discoveries. They stressed that individuals have an immediate and personal relationship with God; and that this is the source of faith which brings freedom from external constraint. This individualism, in turn, led to a vision of a collective independence in which states and nations asserted their independence of and freedom from Rome. Such a theology soon found a fertile reception amid the already emergent merchant classes who had discovered that individual initiative opened up new ways of creating wealth. It is quite remarkable that the power of such a simple idea did not lead to an entirely unbridled individualism in which the more successful exploited the weak more than they did. The reason for this can also be found in the Reformation theology. A sense of individual moral responsibility went alongside this belief in individual freedom and this, in turn, made the Reformation teaching morally earnest in the sense that individuals became keenly aware of their responsibility for one another's welfare. All this was the essence of the Protestant ethic. It matched ideally the moral character which was required in the new mercantile conditions and, as is well known, contributed directly to their phenomenal success. Capitalism, as it came to be known, cannot exist outside a moral framework which provides social stability, truth telling and promise keeping. Little wonder that the Protestant ethic was so much a part of its emergence.

A seminal pastoral expression of this new individualism is to be found in the Lutheran notion of 'the care of all for the souls of all' in which, literally, all care for the souls of all. Its corollary the 'priesthood of all believers', created Christian communities in which mutual care and support, even correction, could enable individuals to work out, not just their own salvation, but also the extent of their responsibility for the salvation of others. This was expressed, for example, in the rules of membership of the Augustana Synod: 'members shall lead a Christian life in charity, humility, and peace. Endeavouring through admonition, consolation and encouragement to edify one another in the faith.'[1] Such emphasis on individual responsibility, in turn, had a profound influence on Reformation doctrines of the Church which gave prominence to lay involvement and responsibility. This was particularly true of the Pietist churches and others influenced by them, notably, in the United Kingdom, the Methodist churches. They too gave central roles to individual believers with clearly defined pastoral responsibilities. The early 'Rules for Helpers' in Methodism, along with the 'Band' and 'Class' systems of meeting created, in a short space of time, both a lay theology and a practical framework in which lay spirituality and ministry could be instructed and flourish. The subsequent introduction of an ordained ministry in Methodism (initially against the will of John Wesley), complicated this and still does so. But the Methodist tradition stands as a clear example of a Church with a high doctrine of individual lay spirituality and pastoral responsibility of a sort which was established by the Protestant Reformation.

This emphasis on individualism was further strengthened by the eighteenth-century Enlightenment and the effect which that, in turn, came to have on Protestant religion. It, too, encouraged individuals to challenge authority, no matter how impervious it may have appeared to be. In England, the Reform Movement, begun by Jeremy Bentham and others, much of which came to statute in the Reform Bill of 1832, marks the political outworking of the Enlightenment assertion of individual autonomy and judgement. Similarly, in eighteenth-century philosophy, the knowing individual is given precedence over what is known. This is most evident in the philosophy of Kant, which claimed that what is known cannot transcend the limits of the knower's experience. This was his, so-called, 'Copernican Revolution' in philosophy. It made the objects of knowledge conform to the knowing subject and not vice versa as had been previously believed. Kant had a great influence on the philosophy of Karl Marx and the theology of Friedrich Schleiermacher, for whom the foundation of true spirituality was to be found deep in the individual's sense of dependence upon God. For this reason, Schleiermacher is often described as the Father of modern theology. He magisterially interpreted the theological implications of late eighteenth-century philosophical discoveries and did so in such a way that the majority of nineteenth-century Protestant theologians were influenced by his work.

This, of course, is only an outline of the story of the place of individualism in Protestant theology. It is important to note for our purpose so that we can be reminded why it is that the one-to-one care of individuals in the Protestant tradition is an inseparable part of its theology and philosophy. In this way, a unique value was placed on every individual soul before God. Pastoral theology is, therefore, greatly enriched by the study of individualism in the Protestant reformed tradition and of how it has been brought to bear on pastoral ministry and practice. This will remain an important aspect of pastoral theology proper, even though, as we shall see in the next chapter, it is incomplete without paying equal attention to the social dimensions of human welfare.

The historic emphasis on individualism in Protestantism has been congenial to the twentieth-century attention to the pastoral welfare of individuals in numerous psychoanalytic theories and movements. Until very recently, at least, they too have been preoccupied with the care and welfare of individuals. Indeed, these modern secular theories all share the presupposition, largely under the common influence of Freud, that improvements in the human condition come principally from one-to-one in-depth analysis of the experience of the individually counselled by the counsellor. Modern schools of psychotherapy differ in their methods of analysis as well as their treatments. Their proximity to medical practice has had the effect of endowing them with a clinical ethos. This is clear from the way in which the counsellor/counselled relationship is often a mirror of the doctor/patient one. This relationship is, for example, governed by arranged set-time appointments in which the counsellor is expected to take initiatives, control the process and discover the nature of the condition as well as administer a cure. The many different schools of psychotherapy have also shared a belief that the whole process is value-free, in the sense that it is ostensibly conducted in a secular environment without reference to either religion or secular ideology.

All such activity, however, remains heavily value-laden implicitly or explicitly. One explicit explanation of such values has drawn on the notion of 'human growth and development' or 'self-actualization'.[2] This holds the view that the resources of human welfare are all to be found within human experience. We shall later see that this is an issue for debate for those engaged in counselling from a Christian point of view, but before we turn to an examination of that, we will first consider in more detail some of the modern methods used in the care of individuals. In general, modern secular counselling has derived from Freudian psychoanalysis the belief that counselling can be used both to diagnose disorders as well as treat them. In a later development, drug therapy has sometimes been used in the cure stage as an adjunct to psychoanalysis rather than as an integral or necessary part of it. To understand a little of what all the modern therapies have in common it will, therefore, first be necessary to consider Freudian views of psychoanalysis.

Sigmund Freud and his successors

Freud's interest in psychology was prompted by a desire to find a cure for hysteria. He combined his natural curiosity with the experimental treatment of patients. The contact between counsellor and clients, accordingly, had to be regular, intense and, if necessary, prolonged indefinitely. He used a process of relaxed free association in which the client, lying supine, was encouraged to reply to his questions, preferably without hesitation or conscious thought. The reason for this is that he placed a great deal of importance on the distinction between the conscious and unconscious mind.

This holds that at any time we know that we know certain things, that is, we are conscious of them. But we are also, at any given time, aware that we know things of which we are not immediately conscious. Moreover, the total content of the unconscious is constantly lurking beneath the conscious surface of our minds in such a way that it presents a threat to it. This is why, according to Freud, we instinctively repress our own unconscious minds, allowing out of them only what we know we can consciously control. This repression of the unconscious is a dynamic force. It is largely self-operating, in the sense that its constant vigilance is a part of the unconscious process which it mysteriously guards. Under normal circumstances, this process operates automatically and has no observably adverse effects on the health of an individual. But, if there is something in the unconscious which is threatening the conscious mind, then conscious repression automatically asserts itself. This often presents itself as an obsessional preoccupation with neurotic symptoms.

Freud thought that the most common cause of such neuroses was the obsession with primal sexual impulses. Accordingly, he formulated his theory 'that among other things I suspect the following: that hysteria is conditioned by a primary sexual experience (before puberty) accompanied by revulsion and fright; and that obsessional neurosis is conditioned by the same accompanied by pleasure'.[3] This insight provided the sole basis for Freud's more considered view that hysteria and the neurosis it generates arise from sexual experience before puberty in which shock and pleasure gives rise to guilt and repression, as distinct from neurosis not generated by hysteria in which guilt is caused entirely by conscious activities. Freud was attempting several things at once. The treatment of patients; the formulation of a theory of the mind which would explain the hysterical condition; and the articulation of a conscious and unconscious psychology of neurosis. His critics have frequently highlighted the unscientific nature of his theories and it has been suggested that, far from reading off his theories from his observations and experiments, he made the latter fit the preconceived theories. In so doing, the criticism continues, he used a process that was more akin to intuitive imagining than scientific deduction.[4]

Freud's research, however, gave rise to two disciplines: psychoanalysis and psychotherapy. Psychoanalysis now claims to have amassed a wealth of scientific and respectable evidence in support of its central claims, but it began with Freud's more primitive work. The psychotherapist, like the analyst, works with a direct and personal contact with the 'patient'. The method used is one of dialogue and, as different psychotherapies have emerged, they have developed their own distinctive, so-called, 'Neo-Freudian' methods. The term cannot properly allow for the extent of innovation achieved by the newer psychotherapies which have moved far away from their Freudian beginnings. These are associated with the names of Adler, Rank, Sullivan and Fromm. Rogers, as we shall see, developed his views separately. These newer psychotherapies have all, in their own way, been critical of the extent to which Freud emphasized the importance of instinctual drives, such as the libido. Alternatively, they have stressed the importance of examining environmental factors and influences. 'Neo-Freudian man is clearly a less driven creature, more directly in touch with his environment, less demonic and more hopeful'.[5] Many of these later therapies, however, still share Freud's preoccupation with sexuality. One example is Wilhelm Reich who focused on conscious rather than unconscious sexual desires and advocated 'biofunctional' therapy.[6] Not surprisingly, this gave an even greater prominence to sexuality than was given by Freud. Such variations on Freud's original work proliferate and people turn to them in considerable numbers in search of solutions to personal problems, although there are now indications that the vogue for such counselling may be on the wane.

A *genre* of popular self-help literature such as T. A. Harris' *I'm O.K., You're O.K.,*[7] and M. Newman and B. Berkowitz' *How to Be Your Own Best Friend*[8] have also been popularly influential in twentieth-century psychotherapy. This popularity may partly be due to two factors. First, although medicine is phenomenally successful in prolonging life and often at prolonging active life, it cannot eradicate the worry of disease and illness as a source of genuine anxiety among the healthy. One pastoral effect of this is that a 'faith' in modern medicine, which supposed that it alone could provide for the total welfare of human beings, is now considerably eroded. Of course, it may, rightly, be observed that such faith if it did exist, was seriously misplaced to begin with. The second possible reason why the psychotherapies have become so popular might have to do with the perceived demise of religion as a source of solace for the seriously troubled. This does not mean that all who seek psychotherapy turn away from religion because, as we shall see, religious counsellors have themselves used psychoanalysis and therapy in their work. But to those for whom religion offers no solace, psychotherapy has obvious attractions.

Modern psychotherapies can be grouped under three headings. First, those which emphasize cognitive and emotional processes, an example of which is transactional analysis, which came to notice following the publication of Eric Berne's *Games People Play*.[9] Its popularity was greatly enhanced, some years later, with the appearance of Harris' already mentioned book which sold over a million copies. Berne was trained as a Freudian analyst and worked out a structured way of analysing and controlling the way people interact in groups. This included the study of environmental and emotional stimuli; 'strokes', as elements of the transaction between group members. Some groups were led in a non-directive way and some were overtly erotic and sexual in their activity. What they all sought was a therapeutic equilibrium in the interactive group relationships. Gestalt therapy, and family therapy, are further popular examples of therapies in this first group. The emphasis here is directed away from cerebral insight, although that is not denied, to an activity which ascribes a central role to bodily sensation. Members of these groups are therapeutically encouraged to pay attention to immediate bodily sensations and needs. The ease with which this could develop into a preoccupation with sexual sensation and desire is obvious.

The second group of therapies are those which arise from the first and which emphasize, even further, the importance of bodily activity and behavioural processes. Examples are the sexual therapies of Masters and Johnson and other attempts at behavioural modification and assertion training.[10] The third group of therapies take this even further by emphasizing the importance of understanding and controlling biological processes. Psychedelic drugs are sometimes used to achieve this.

Individual psychotherapies such as these have been, as we have noted, extremely popular. A simple factor may partly account for this, namely the inconvenience of convening therapeutic groups for the required long periods. By contrast, one-to-one arrangements are more easily made and sustained. Also, suspicions have arisen that many therapeutic groups have had the unintended effect of inducing artificially the very symptoms they were ostensibly trying to cure. In other words, the groups themselves became inducing agents, causing their members to behave in ways which were not necessarily correlative with the ways they behaved outside them. Yet a further criticism holds that some groups may have produced artificial conditions of dependence in which, alone, the needs of their members can be met and on which they come to rely inordinately. Indeed, a more severe criticism would be that many groups do not recognize the moral obligations they have towards their members for the way the group activity affects life beyond the group. For all these possible criticisms of some group activity, however, they are and will remain attractive to those who need a level of therapeutic contact with others which one-to-one counselling cannot offer. Moreover, groups are showing themselves ever capable of adapting to new needs. For these reasons alone they will remain important. Their educational, or re-educational, uses such as those with addicts and alcoholics are now widely and successfully established. The value of this is, again, shown by the proliferation of self-help groups which seek to cater for the special needs of people who find themselves comforted and instructed by the opportunity to meet others with virtually identical needs and who may have become more experienced at coping with them. Many of the more established such self-help groups have become important politically as they have lobbied for the interests and needs of their members.

Thus far we have seen how the preoccupation with the care of individuals has a particular history which can be traced to both religious and philosophical roots. The Protestant tradition made the individual central to its story of salvation; the philosophers made the individual central to their understanding of knowledge.

Freud's work should be seen in this context. He was, likewise, strongly focused on the individual, or, more precisely, by the individual psychotic condition. As we have seen, albeit with different emphases, others followed him by doing much the same thing. Whilst Freud was interested in religion, he considered it an illusion on the grounds that it did not admit of proof. Nor, as we have also seen for that matter, did his own theories. What he fundamentally overlooked was the fact that religion is not simply the beliefs held, rightly or wrongly, by individuals, but more importantly their collective, shared history and communal participation in its continuation through worship and ritual. His own 'scientific' criticisms of these traditions, moreover, failed to appreciate their subtlety and sheer staying power. Subsequent to his work, they have survived and become appreciated in more refined ways. We have seen, throughout, that the locus of religious pastoral need is in shared experiences, particularly those which precipitate a crisis of confidence in hitherto unquestioned certainties. Religion functions at this point with a sophistication which goes beyond the narrow perceptions of individual need as understood by Freud, and equally goes beyond the purview of what he thought was or was not scientific. In religious matters Freud adopted, early in his life, a stance of polemical atheism. As a consequence, his opinions on the subject were pedantically dismissive and they prevented him from even entertaining the idea that human welfare was bound up with the subtleties of collective experiences which religions address in large measure.

Counselling

Counselling and psychotherapy are often used as interchangeable terms, particularly in the USA. It has been noted that, in Britain, the two activities are more separate but not always for clear reasons.[11] In general, it may be observed that pastoral counselling is a more diffuse activity than that of the psychotherapies. It is so for several reasons. Its aims and objectives are often less clearly defined and it engages with a wider range of people from different backgrounds who all become involved for different reasons. Indeed, the very widespread and variant nature of pastoral counselling leads to a frequent desire by pastoral counsellors to sharpen and professionalize their identity. To this end, they have set up methods of training and accreditation as a means of certifying certain individuals or organizations as being qualified to practise as counsellors and/or to train others to do so.[12] Part of the need for this professionalization of counselling lies in the desire to emulate the human sciences, such as the psychotherapies we have been briefly discussing. One system for the accreditation of pastoral counselling is that created by the Clinical Pastoral Education Movement in the USA. This publishes clearly defined requirements which counsellors have to meet and maintain in order to describe themselves as such. When an attempt was made to create a single organization such as this in the UK, in the early 1970s, it was strongly opposed by a number of people, including the influential R. A. Lambourn, a pastoral theologian with medical training, on the grounds that it appropriated an undesirable type of professionalism.[13] Conversely, Lambourn argued for approaches which were deliberately diffuse, encouraged lay people, and eschewed any notion of them being qualified in some way for the purpose. An association was formed, The Association of Pastoral Care and Counselling and, although it does possess a means of accreditation, no extensive use has yet been made of this.

People seeking religious pastoral counselling represent a large proportion of those involved. They have variously seen counselling as a means of evangelism, a means of effecting pastoral care, a means of showing the secular world the acceptability of what they do, and as a means of fulfilling the New Testament pastoral obligation to 'bear one another's burdens' (Gal 6.2). There is much that is congenial to religion in all this. Counselling creates intimate pastoral relationships which can make great demands on all who take part. Referring to this, Charles Curran comments:

> Counselling at its deepest level is both a profound relationship between the self and another and an intensely searching and probing

dialogue ... The relationship between client and counsellor is unquestioningly one of deep emotional and somatic significance, but it is most of all a dynamism of the giving or withholding of the selves of both client and counsellor.[14]

For those who are inspired to counsel, or be counselled, because of their religious beliefs, there is much in those beliefs to draw upon. They enable the examination of the human condition in the light of the great themes of religion: sin and the need for grace and forgiveness. Exploring this, Edward Thurneysen argued in *A Theology of Pastoral Care* that there are two levels of pastoral talk, the purpose of which is to communicate the word of God to individuals as a ministry alongside those of preaching and the sacraments.[15] To speak pastorally, at one level, is to engage in secular discussion in preparation for bringing it into a relationship with the word of God. At the first level, all the secular disciplines of psychology and sociology are used in the attempt to solve human problems. But all this, he stressed, is incomplete unless it is raised to the second level which is that of pastoral conversation. This raises secular counselling to the level of divine discourse where grace, forgiveness and reconciliation are brought to bear on the human condition. This view of Thurneysen's is, perhaps, a somewhat crude one, and it only makes any real sense in the light of the theological influence of his fellow pastor Karl Barth, but it stands as one attempt to show how profound human care leads through pastoral conversation to an awareness of the presence of God, or at least to an awareness of one interpretation of that presence.

   The now extensive modern literature on Christian pastoral counselling was influentially inaugurated by Seward Hiltner with the publication of *Pastoral Counselling* in 1949. Hiltner argues that the aims of pastoral counselling are

the same as those of the Church itself – bringing people to Christ and the Christian fellowship, aiding them to acknowledge and repent of sin and to accept God's freely offered salvation, helping them to live with themselves and their fellow men in brotherhood and love, enabling them to act with faith and confidence instead of the previous doubt and anxiety, bringing peace where discord reigned before.[16]

Experienced pastors, however, will observe that pastoral counselling is seldom clear cut, either in its aims or its achievements. So often, profound pastoral need is only met at the equally profound level of the spirit whose workings are not always scrutable to counselling theories. That, however, is no reason for not attempting to perfect them, in the hope that they will at their best approximate a knowledge of the divine presence in human need.

Following Hiltner, much has been published on the role of counselling in the work of Christian ministers. Some of it has sounded a cautionary note such, for example, as R. S. Lee's *Principles of Pastoral Counselling*. Lee recognizes that, because ministers have to preach the gospel and celebrate the sacraments, they are heavily committed to a functional public role and this may well come into conflict with counselling which requires conversely the creation of intimate personal relationships:

> If he (*sic*) tries to make the switch from one role to another which he feels is incompatible with it, it is almost impossible for him to be sincere and he is bound to fail. Such a minister ought not to attempt counselling. He can give pastoral care which may be very fruitful but it will be of the paternal type.[17]

Following this caution, Lee does express the hope that training in counselling would become an essential part of the training of all ministers. But this is a hope which has manifestly not been fulfilled. Many ministers, however, will counsel naturally and informally, and most easily so with people who are like themselves in religious preference and disposition. This is, in fact, what usually happens, simply because congregations tend to attract people of like mind. Others will not counsel in the formal sense at all and it may be better that they do not, leaving them free to concentrate their energies, rather, on the wider work of the ministry. This does not exclude the obvious possibility that some ministers, given training, as Lee argues, can and will make excellent counsellors. In 1982, Michael Jacobs produced the first edition of *Still Small Voice*, in a successful attempt to build on the work of Lee. This has now been revised and updated in the light of what he calls the 'increased sophistication of those learning counselling in the 1990s'.[18]

In retrospect, the whole post-Second World War debate about ministry and counselling might be seen as one with a hidden agenda about authority. Does the counselling movement *per se* present a threat to the authority of the Christian ministry? Is it too fanciful to interpret the willingness of that ministry to participate in counselling as a response at least in part to that threat? If so, then the admonitions of Lambourn and others may point to a need for a recovery of ministerial confidence which can achieve the aims of counselling without aspiring to the imprimatur of formalized practices, structures and qualifications. No small part of such a recovery will come from a heightened sense of the relationship between contemporary counselling methods and the older traditional insights of Christianity. The need to bring modern pastoral methods into a relationship with traditional ones is, as we are seeing, a recurrent one. It is what helps to give Christian pastoral ministry its identity. This is not an exclusive identity. It draws, at times, on non-Christian sources, but what it cannot do is to forget, or deny, the identity of its own past.

An important analysis of the role of such identity in pastoral counselling was made by Paul Halmos in *The Faith of the Counsellors*, first published in 1965. Halmos observed the then phenomenal increase in counselling activity and, with it, the increase of the counsellor's influence on society. As a sociologist, he attempted to explain why this was the case and suggested that it was because of a widespread and growing scepticism about any real possibility of bringing about any lasting political betterment of the human lot, which has driven people to seek this betterment instead by individual and personal means. Halmos observes of counsellors in general, that they were reticent about the first principles of their work.[19] Such principles, that is, which would explain why counselling is undertaken, how it is sustained and to what end. All that could be discovered was derived from what he thought to be but scant accounts of psychological theory and psychoanalysis. This, observes Halmos, displays a tender mindedness and an unbecoming reticence. This does not mean that counsellors are incapable of exercising moral discipline and selflessness, on the contrary, they often do so. But it points to an unacceptable refusal to be clear about first principles, thereby leaving some of the most important features of their work unexplained. Halmos argues that:

> The counsellor applies himself in a way which suggests a set of convictions, a powerful mood, a moral stance, a faith. To call this exercise an outcome of faith is, I believe, well warranted for it has many of the characteristics of human experience and behaviour with which we associate the notion of faith.[20]

This faith is, he further argues, paradoxically related to the claim made by counsellors that the methods and contents of their work were derived from scientifically based observations and insights. The counsellors, by this means, became a moral–cultural élite of their age, claiming the alleged benefits of science and combining them with the more ancient religious images of themselves as comforters. Halmos' work is an important attempt to analyse the elements of this paradox. He concludes that 'the counsellor's practice and theory depend upon assumptions and value judgements, which have a potent influence not only on his work, but also on the culture of the society in which the counsellor works'.[21] For this reason, counselling has an obligation to explain itself. Halmos has shown the shallowness of the claim that what it does is value-free, whilst noting the extent to which some forms of counselling have elevated this insight to a central position.[22] He did recognize that certain degrees of clinical detachment are sometimes necessary, especially when individual counsellors have large case-loads. What the stress on faith shows, however, is that total clinical detachment is, in fact, impossible. Halmos only tentatively explores how pre-existing faiths may work themselves out through the insights of psychoanalysis and counselling. The engagement of the Christian faith with individual counselling has a profundity for the reasons explained at the beginning of this chapter. Its insights into individual well-being, which are derived from theological beliefs in the inestimable divine worth of every human being, enable counselling to be used to restore the divine image in human lives wherever it is marred for whatever reason. Christian counsellors need to be as clear about their Christianity as they need to be about the principles of their counselling. In the end, however, counselling is not susceptible of entirely rational explanation since it deals with the essential mysteries of human well-being. Halmos draws attention to this when he talks of counselling being paradoxical. What religiously motivated counselling does is to bring a vision of human worth to bear on the needs of the counselled in the belief that these needs are capable of redemption by grace. It often does this, moreover, in the context of prayer both with and for the counselled. Above all, religiously centred counselling is counselling with a purpose and to the extent in which it is so, it is clearly directive. For this reason it runs counter to another influential movement in modern counselling which has elevated the need to be non-directive to the status of a sacred principle.

This movement is associated, principally, with the lifetime's work of Carl Rogers and is arguably America's first indigenous approach to counselling. Rogers reacted against all the Freudian schools of psychotherapy, on the grounds that they placed individuals in a preconceived schema. This, felt Rogers, compromised individuality by expecting individuals to respond to assumptions which might be totally inappropriate to their particular condition. Influenced by Liberal Protestantism, and the congenial liberal educational philosophies of Dewey and others, Rogers countered the

Freudian-based psychotherapies with a view that established the inviolable status of the client as a person who should be understood independently of both psychoanalytic theory and her or his environment. To this end, he established the use of the word 'client' in preference to the Freudian use of 'patient' to stress that those who were so called did not, in seeking help, diminish any of their own freedom and responsibility. This, he believed was precisely what was abrogated in Freudian and Neo-Freudian psychotherapies. This marks a break with the Freudian therapies which religiously motivated counsellors found conducive. Rogers works with a clear view of who persons are, but it is, however, very different from what any religious counsellors might uncritically want to accept. For him, persons are isolated individuals who possess, entirely within their own resources, the means of their own healing. For this reason he can be seen as an exemplar of the humanist approach to therapy. And, as we shall see, it is the conflict of this humanism with more Christian approaches which can invoke the sort of paradox of which Halmos speaks. Rogers argues that within every individual there is a whole person with infinite potential to order his or her own life, free from external influences. Accordingly, the point of counselling is to enable the individual to become whole, and to do so of their own volition.

Such a view is best understood as part of the widespread North American 'human growth and potential' movement. This movement is an amalgam of existentialist attitudes to the person, and the all-pervading North American belief in the potentially infinite perfectibility of every individual. Throughout his distinguished career, Rogers has examined the relevance of these views of human nature for psychotherapy. Work he did during the period 1938–50, when he laid the foundation for all that was to follow, was summed up in his *Client Centred Therapy* (1951).[23] Since then he has stressed that the term 'person-centred' therapy is applicable to all individuals, even those who do not consider themselves eligible for, or in need of, formal counselling.[24] This, he argues, makes the notion applicable to the work of other groups, many of which may be only obliquely therapeutic, if at all. Examples are groups promoting political and educational activities. The presupposition here is that all individuals fall short of the realization of their true potential. In *A Way of Being* (1980) Rogers set the insight of his earlier work in a wider social and political context, in response no doubt to criticisms which were made of it by those who thought these dimensions to be lacking.[25]

Whilst Rogers was more open to the social and political dimensions of counselling in his later work, the influence of his earlier views remains. Note that the fundamental precept of person-centred therapy is that every individual is essentially good and infinitely self-perfectible. The corollary of this view is that all external influences which impede the growth and development of an individual can only be controlled by the individual. It is interesting to observe here that Rogers is, in fact, engaging in a much older and ongoing debate about human nature. Against all claims to the contrary, Rogers doggedly insists that human nature is positive, forward-moving constructive, realistic and trustworthy. Because of this, what the counsellor should do, according to Rogers, is to form an unobtrusive enabling relationship with the client. This is achieved by the counsellor trying to empathize with the client to such a degree that she or he comes to know something of that person's unique, by definition, view of themselves and the world. It is, therefore, the counsellor's task to understand something of

> the internal frame of reference of the client, to perceive the world as the client sees it, to perceive the client himself as seen by himself, to lay aside all perceptions from the external frame of reference while doing so, and to communicate something of the empathetic understanding to the client.[26]

Most importantly, this can only be achieved by genuine dialogue which requires the total personal interaction of the counsellor with the person. This requires the counsellor to be non-judgmental, non-reactive and, indeed, totally passive in her or his encounter with the other person. The hand that guides here is an invisible one, since any visibility would compromise the fundamental principles of Roger's approach. The hope is that through a process of self-initiated change, the person counselled will gradually realize his or her own true potential, and in doing so be oblivious of having received any guidance from another. Indeed, at its best, this approach should not require direct guidance from another at all. All that can be allowed is that the counsellor will heighten the person's awareness of her or his own experience and, as a result, enable them to improve their condition.

Rogers studied the existentialist writers Kierkegaard, Buber and Sartre and, although he claimed that he was unaware of being under any direct influence from them, his work, nevertheless, shows important points of agreement with them particularly on the understanding of personhood.[27] For example, they all assert that personal experience precedes theoretical construction, in the sense that what is given in experience is to be interpreted independently of any theory into which it might be integrated. They all emphasize the unique worth of the individual, the primacy of individual perception and, most importantly, they all locate the power to change things in individual agency. The affinity between these views and those of Rogers is clear.

What are we to make of this from the point of view of Christian pastoral theology? What is to be the result of a 'conversation' between the views of Rogers and Christian tradition? The faith that so inheres for Rogers is one which places a great deal of trust in the innate ability of human beings to act as the agency of their own betterment. Everything else Rogers says about counselling hinges on this central element of *faith*. As we saw in Chapter 2, existentialist views of the human person are important to the extent in which they enable us to focus on the power of individual agency and, in so doing, value the infinite worth of every individual person. This needs to be especially remembered whenever collectivism obscures it. Movingly this was what did happen after 1945 in the Nuremberg Trials. The widespread and deep horror of Nazism did much to create a receptive popular culture for the post-war existentialism of writers such as Sartre and Camus. The point they repeatedly made in popular form was that all integrity should be based on individual integrity.

The existentialist view of human nature and agency is, however, flawed when, as it invariably does, it overlooks the interdependence of individuals with each other. The Christian understanding of individualism can embrace some of the existentialist view of the same, but it breaks from it when it stresses its view that individuals are persons-in-relation. First, persons are in relation to God their Creator and second they are in relation to one another. These relationships enjoin them to care for one another by assuming, under God, total responsibility for one another to the point even of self-sacrifice. The great metaphors of the New Testament, in general, and the writings of St Paul in particular are, as we have seen, redolent with explorations of the nature of the human–divine and the human–human interdependence. To the extent to which Rogerian psychotherapy does not recognize this, it must be judged, from the Christian point of view, to be inadequate. Whilst they might appreciate existentialist understandings of the individual for the important corrective that they are to other unacceptable views, Christians must, nevertheless, conclude that the understanding of personhood in their own tradition is the more profound. This, again, is a good illustration of just how Christian tradition engages in critical conversation with contemporary culture and thought and, in so doing, transforms it.

The unexamined belief in the innate goodness of human nature which is found in some existentialist writers also runs counter to Christian insights into original sin and the need it creates for grace and forgiveness. Rogers, as we have seen, was an heir to nineteenth-century liberalism and recognized its easy conflation with the North American dream of infinite progress. This does not enable him to appreciate the real nature of human culpability. The understanding of this is, by contrast, at the heart of the Christian understanding of personhood. The Christian claim is that human nature is flawed and that the flaw resides not so much in the ability to acquire knowledge, but in the ability to put knowledge into effect. 'For I do not the good I want, but the evil I do not want is what I do' (Rom 7.19). This is the profundity of the Christian view of the person. By contrast, in classical pre-Christian thought (for example that of Plato), it was believed that virtue could actually be increased by acquiring knowledge. This is why, of course, he believed that every king should be a philosopher. Such a view often still persists in opposition to Christianity. Against this view, Christianity asserts that complete virtue is available to sinful human beings only as a result of their ability to receive God's grace in contrition and forgiveness of their sins. A view which is very different from that of Rogers who holds, as we have seen, that human nature is infinitely self-perfectible.

The Christian counsellor, in further criticism of Rogers, will also hold that it is not always possible for her or him to function as an unseen non-directive hidden influence. Christian counsellors may well want to learn from Rogerian therapy all the important things it says about empathy and about how to help individuals to help themselves, but they cannot always leave it there. Much Christian pastoral care is directive, in the sense that it draws on the insights of Christian tradition to illuminate the present. Extreme existentialist-type alternatives to this can represent a sort of 'presentism' which arrogantly assumes that the present situation is not only different from whatever has gone before, it also has to regard whatever has been done before as in principle untrustworthy. There may well be, of course, novel elements to present dilemmas but to suppose, in principle, that the past never has anything to say, or more particularly suppose that those with a knowledge of the past never have anything to say, is to epitomize the arrogance of presentism. In opposing this, however, it is well for Christians to remember that there are equally arrogances awaiting them if they fail to recognize the importance of the present even to the point of allowing that it may well, if necessary, require them to rethink the yield of past insight. At the very least, Christian understanding of the past can be incorrect and in need of revision. This, for example, has been shown to be the case in attitudes to slavery in the nineteenth century, to feminism in the twentieth and increasingly to homosexuality in the present.

More acceptably from a Christian point of view, as we shall see in the next chapter, post-Rogerian therapies have tended, for a variety of reasons, to emphasize the importance of the social dimensions of human well-being. Transactional analysis, gestalt and family therapies, for example, have all acknowledged the importance of exploring the social dimension of human need. But before we turn to consider that, one more thing needs to be noted about the significance of the counselling movements for pastoral theology. That is the way in which they have generated insights into the counselling of persons with specific afflictions and conditions. These specific applications of counselling are identified by looking at some of the needs of those who benefit from them. Indeed, the arrival of some unprecedented need may itself require the development of an entirely new form of counselling application. Counselling those who are afflicted with the HIV virus is an obvious and tragic example of this. Others examples are to be found in the need for specialist counselling which communities require after they experience sudden traumas. There is a growing appreciation of the relevance and value of the special counselling skills which can be used in such tragic circumstances, notwithstanding the probably justified cautions which ought to be observed, which might well show that counselling has a tendency to be supply-led in the sense that if it is there people will suppose they need it.

Quite often those with specific needs set about organizing their own self-help groups, if they cannot get the help they need from elsewhere. Many such now exist and they often facilitate a form of co-counselling in which shared need becomes the foundation for profound empathy leading to the exchange of valuable psychological support and practical information. There are now so many of these groups and their successes are so well established that their place in the counselling movement is assured. Not because they are necessarily professional in the sense of being formally qualified, they are invariably not, but because they are remarkably effective in achieving their aims. All we can do here is to select some of them and discuss them briefly as examples of others.

Whilst common needs do not always manifest themselves in identical ways, they can be generally classified. Examples are family counselling, health counselling, crisis counselling, rehabilitation counselling, community counselling, career counselling, referral counselling, supportive counselling, confrontational counselling, grief counselling, marriage counselling, and sexual counselling. The endless nature of the list alone shows how widespread the specialist counselling movements have become. Many such specialist counselling applications can be sub-divided; crisis counselling, for example, may be divided into counselling applications which deal with certain sorts of crises: for example, rape, unemployment, physical attack. Virtually all areas of specialist counselling can be sub-divided in this way.

Some counsellors may, of course, be more suited to some applications of counselling rather than others. Some, moreover, may be suited by dint of their own experiences and, in passing the benefit of them on to others, may well be strengthened in their own endeavours to cope. Alcoholics Anonymous groups are particularly successful at enabling their members to achieve this. In many of these areas, specialist agencies exist to select and train people for specific types of counselling work. The Samaritans, for example, are particularly noted for their achievements in this area.

The widespread existence of such specialist counselling raises interesting questions about the relationship of theory to practice in counselling. For the most part, specialist counsellors are comparatively untrained and certainly, even if they receive some basic training, they remain amateurs. Whilst there are areas of counselling where the strictest professional training is necessary, in psychiatry, for example, by far the greater part of all effective pastoral care is provided by untrained or minimally trained counsellors, as we noted in Chapter 1. They are no less obliged, of course, to give an account of themselves than professional counsellors are. For this reason their *faith* and the methods they use must receive equal scrutiny. Many who are less than confident of their methods and presuppositions will, perhaps, be more open to meeting the ordinary or extraordinary needs of others. Here the theories will be less directly applicable or even obvious, but they cannot be disregarded completely, since any who aspire to help others in organized ways should always be prepared to give an account of themselves.

Brief articles with bibliographies on specific applications of counselling can be found in *A Dictionary of Pastoral Care*.[28] These are cross-referenced to related issues. A now classic discussion of some of the applications of counselling can be found in H. J. Clinebell's *Basic Types of Pastoral Care and Counselling*[29] formerly *Basic Types of Pastoral Counselling*. This is written explicitly from the point of view of Christian pastoral counselling and, in particular, from that of ministerial counselling, although there is a chapter on the place of pastoral counselling in lay ministry. These two texts when used together will provide a more than adequate introduction to counselling in its specific applications. A more detailed study is Gary S. Belkin's *Introduction to Counselling*, part four of which is devoted to counselling applications.[30]

Clearly, then, the Christian tradition has a great deal to contribute to the contemporary understanding of the care of individuals.[31] First, we have noted the Christian roots of the concept of the 'individual'. It is grounded in the Reformation understanding of personal salvation. Second, we have challenged certain assumptions made about people. They should not be viewed in isolation; and the sinful side of being human should be taken seriously.

This is the transforming model at work. In 'conversation' with Christ and the Christian tradition, modernity is neither accepted nor rejected uncritically. In an ongoing process it becomes folded into and, by that means, a part of older insights and traditions. We will now turn to a consideration of whether or not Christian tradition can similarly transform our understanding of the pastoral care of societies.

Notes

1   Quoted by McNeill, J. T. (1977) *A History of the Cure of Souls*, p. 191. New York: Harper & Row.
2   See Frick, W. B. (1971) *Humanistic Psychology*, Colombus, Ohio: Charles Merrill.
3   Quoted by Ibister, J. M. (1985) *Freud, An Introduction to His Life and Work*, p. 70. London: Polity Press.
4   See Fisher, Seymour and Greenburg, Robert P. (1977) *The Scientific Credibility of Freud's Theories and Therapy*, Hassocks: Harvester Press. See also Jacobs, M. (1992) *Sigmund Freud*, London: Sage Publications.
5   Koval, Joel (1976) *A Complete Guide to Therapy*, p. 125. Harmondsworth: Pelican Books.
6   Reich, Wilhelm (1949) *Character Analysis*, New York: Farrarr Straus, Giroux.
7   Harris, T. A. (1969) *I'm O.K., You're O.K.*, New York: Avon.
8   Berkowitz, B. and Newman, M. (1986) *How to Be Your Own Best Friend*, Newark: Ballantine.
9   Berne, E. (1968) *Games People Play*, London: Penguin.
10 Masters, W. and Johnson, V. (1966) *Human Sexual Response*, Boston: Little Brown.
11 Campbell, Alastair V., ed. (1987) *A Dictionary of Pastoral Care*, p. 56. London: SPCK. This volume is now an indispensable reference work.
12 Ibid., p. 3.
13 Ibid.
14 Arbuckle, D. S., ed. (1967) *Counselling and Psychotherapy, An Overview*, p. 54. New York: McGraw-Hill.
15 Thurneysen, E. (1962) *A Theology of Pastoral Care*, pp. 101–78. Richmond: John Knox Press.
16 Hiltner, S. (1949) *Pastoral Counselling*, p. 19. New York: Abingdon.

17 Lee, R. S. (1968) *Principles of Pastoral Counselling*, p. 80. London: SPCK.
18 Jacobs, M. (1993) *Still Small Voice*, p. x. London: SPCK.
19 Halmos, P. (1965) *The Faith of the Counsellors*, p. 4. London: Constable.
20 Ibid., p. 6.
21 Ibid., p. 8.
22 See Delaney, Daniel J. and Eisenberg, Sheldon (1972) *The Counselling Process*, pp. 50–78. Chicago: Rand McNally.
23 Rogers, C. R. (1951) *Client Centred Therapy*. London: Constable.
24 Rogers, C. R. (1980) *A Way of Being*, pp. 114ff. Boston: Houghton Mifflin.
25 Ibid.
26 Rogers, *Client Centred Therapy*, p. 29.
27 See Barclay, James R. (1971) *Foundations of Counselling Strategies*, pp. 336–7. New York: John Wiley & Sons.
28 See note 11 above.
29 Clinebell, H. J. (1984) *Basic Types of Pastoral Care and Counselling*, Nashville: Abingdon.
30 Belkin, G. S., ed. (1984) *Introduction to Counselling*, pp. 297–330. Iowa: Wm. L. Brown. Maria Walke and Michael Jacobs are the series editors of current and forthcoming titles on counselling in its many different contexts by Oxford University Press.
31 Cf. Jacobs, M. (1988) *Towards the Fullness of Christ*, London: Darton, Longman & Todd.

6

Social care

In the last chapter, we explored the traditional model of pastoral theology – the care for the individual. It was shown that one difficulty with the focus on individuals in this way is that it invariably overlooks the extent to which they have to be understood in wider social contexts. When this is done, a wider and richer picture of pastoral theology emerges. One which is argued for throughout this book.

The everyday transition from caring for individuals to caring about their social conditions is so commonplace that it can be taken for granted. There are, however, five stages of it which are worth noting. They commonly occur in case work and all follow from initial one-to-one contact with the cared-for.

(a) They begin when pastors seek help and counsel with those who may be described as 'significant other persons'. These may be members of the family, friends or colleagues. Even here a significant step is taken away from one-to-one caring relationships.

(b) This is taken further when it becomes necessary to mobilize voluntary or statutory assistance, such as in domiciliary care where the needs of the cared-for and immediate family are complemented by help from outside the home. This has now been widely developed as an alternative to more expensive and often less personally acceptable institutional care. It provides often quite simple and very effective forms of help. The Macmillan Nursing Service is just one outstanding example of this. Such involvement of wider community resources inevitably introduces political and economic considerations into pastoral care. The creation and maintenance of even minimum levels of provision of this kind can necessitate a great deal of social and political activity.

(c) Pressure, or self-help, groups are a further stage in the migration of pastoral care from the individual to the social sphere. Such groups are often created by determined founder members in the face of official indifference. As we saw in the last chapter, these groups are particularly successful at bringing together people who care for those in need and have shared interests and experiences, such as parents of handicapped children.

(d) A significantly progressive political step is next taken whenever the relief of need is seen to require a change of public attitude. This can require long-term effort and be expensive to achieve.

(e) Finally, the relief of pastoral need may well require overt social change which can only be brought about by direct political action. An example is the pastoral care for the long-term unemployed. Much can be done to care for their immediate needs, but lasting changes can only be brought about by changing the attitude of governments towards employment policy, and by creating the right economic conditions for increased and sustained employment to be possible.

This last stage of political activity and care appears to be far removed f[r]om one-to-one pastoral care, but there are arguably only four stages of escalating social and political engagement between them. The important point this illustrates is that pastoral care and concern is inescapably political by nature. This does not mean that individual pastors are always necessarily engaged in every stage of political action. That will involve the labours of many who are far removed from the initial pastoral concerns which gave rise to it.

This recognition of the inescapably social nature of pastoral care illustrates the need for pastoral theology to embrace social and political theology.[1]

Social and political theology

Social theology studies the relationship of the knowledge of God to social structures and their bearing on human well-being. A branch of social theology is 'social ethics', which identifies those ethical values which are appropriate for societies to hold.[2] Social theology and ethics have to remember that sin is as much a feature of social as it is of individual life. This is why in social ethics the highest virtue is that of justice, in contrast to individual ethics, where the highest virtue is self-sacrifice. These different sorts of virtue have to be pursued in different ways. This was classically discussed by Reinhold Niebuhr in *Moral Man and Immoral Society*, in which he recognized that love cannot be applied to society without qualification.[3] We will discuss this more fully below. Social theology and social ethics are both part of a wider political theology, a brief consideration of which is necessary before exploring the relationship of pastoral care to societies.

Classically the phrase 'political theology' was taken as being descriptive of any theology which served political ends, such as the preservation of the political *status quo*. St Augustine, for example, largely endorsed this view, but insisted that the true ends of political theology were heavenly rather than earthly. He did this, as we have seen, in his doctrine of the 'two cities', the earthly and the heavenly. The politics of the earthly city had a penultimate relationship with those of the heavenly city. His doctrine of love, with its attempt to fuse *eros* and *agape* in *caritas*, is part of his explanation of the relationship between the two cities.[4] In the Reformation a similar attempt was made by Luther to distinguish the earthly kingdom from the heavenly kingdom. The heavenly kingdom was at God's right hand and the earthly at left. Only God knows the exact relationship between them. In the earthly kingdom he made provision through 'orders' for the well-being of his creatures. These are the state, marriage, the family and work. Lutheran theology became notorious for its political conservatism because it encouraged apolitical forms of piety. Lutherans in the twentieth century were forced to grapple with this legacy. To do this they have had to rework their theology to make it capable of criticizing the state if it becomes necessary to do so. The Lutheran theologian Dietrich Bonhoeffer was one of the most radical of these. He rejected the older Lutheran view that there are unchanging and God-given 'orders' of creation. Instead, he claimed that Christ revealed *mandates* which enable Christians to be socially and politically critical.[5] Bonhoeffer's theology is poignant in the extreme in the light of his own death by execution for the part he played in a failed attempt to assassinate Hitler.

The term 'political theology' first appeared in modern theological writing in the title of Carl Schmitt's *Politische Theologie*.[6] Rather in the classical tradition, Schmitt claimed, broadly, that political authority was derived from a social context which was, in its turn, based on theology. This seemingly mild observation provoked a considerable debate, particularly among theologians who were reluctant to accept that, if it were true, Schmitt's thesis could be taken to imply that theology, in some form at least, lay behind political perversity, as well as behind political virtue. As a result, some theologians set out to sever the link between theology and politics. Chief among these were those influenced by the theology of Karl Barth. They did this by stressing the utter transcendence of God over all human affairs, including politics. Their aim was to show that political perversity was of human and not divine origin. They argued that 'political theology', in the sense that Schmitt has defined it, was an impossibility. It may be observed that the wider historical background of this disagreement, and particularly the rise of Nazism, largely accounted for the nature of the debate and, in particular, for the severity of the Barthian criticism of Schmitt.

Subsequent discussions of political theology have featured in the writings of Johann Baptist Metz,[7] Dorothy Sollë,[8] and Jürgen Moltmann. They have all pointed out, in disagreement with Schmitt, that political theology does provide the means of being critical of political institutions. Moltmann, in particular, claims that it is an essential part of the task of political theology to unmask the pretensions of what he calls the 'political religions', that is, those which tacitly support the political *status quo*.[9] Metz, making the same point, has even suggested that the term 'political theology' ought to be abandoned, because of its conservative overtones, in favour of either calling it 'social' or 'public' theology, but he reluctantly accepts the fact that such a change in nomenclature is unlikely to occur. He stresses the fact that the encounter of individuals with society is more formative for them than the 'I–Thou' encounter which has received so much attention from Buber and others and which, Metz claims, has been responsible for the preservation of a 'privatized' as opposed to a 'social' view of religion. The way in which these points have been taken up in, for example, the liberation theologians, shows that the view that theology needs to be critical of political institutions is now a widely accepted one.[10] But social theology, as such, is far from being a purely modern phenomenon.

Ronald Preston notes that the roots of Anglican social theology and ethics go back to the middle ages.[11] After the Reformation, it continued and, unlike Roman Catholic social theology, was not concerned exclusively with the training of priests. He further notes that it died out towards the end of the seventeenth century for reasons which have never been entirely clarified. As a result, Anglicans had no theological resources they could turn to to deal with the rapidly developing Industrial Revolution and the new pastoral needs it created. Although groups of individuals, such as the early-nineteenth-century Evangelicals of the Clapham Sect, did attack specific social injustices, they did not do so because they had a social theology. Their concern was prompted more by high moral endeavour directed towards specific issues, and perhaps, also, by the realization that the low view of black humanity held by the slave traders ran counter to Christian teaching about the equality of all human beings in the sight of God. As Preston notes, again, it was F. D. Maurice who began the modern non-Roman Catholic rearticulation of a social theology.[12] His particular interest was in the theological and ethical norms which bore on social structures such as work and economic life. Although not developed by Maurice, this reintroduced a prescriptive tone in social theology which became less concerned with how individuals should fit into social structures, but asked, rather, how those structures can best be adapted to meet the needs of individuals. Hence its often markedly revisionary tone. For all these reasons, frequently made superficial comments about it being wrong for churches to 'meddle in politics' reveal a widespread ignorance about the profundity of social and political theology and its place in Christian tradition.

The claim that, because human beings are created in the image of God they only flourish when they are in a right relationship with him and with the presence of his image in others, is central to Christian orthodoxy. It is, moreover, the basis of Christian social thinking. Some would add that the Trinitarian doctrine of God further illustrates the central place given to relational thinking in Christian tradition. The understanding of righteousness is also central to Christian social theology. It is not, primarily at least, a moral concept. It is, rather, a relational one in the sense that it is what follows from establishing a right relationship to God, a relationship which, in its turn, makes morality possible. In this fundamental sense such right relations are a precondition of morality. Establishing them is what Christian spirituality is all about and why there can be no properly Christian thinking about society and morality which is not set in the context of prayer and devotion. This has been well discussed in a recent World Council of Churches publication by Duncan Forrester, *The True Church and Morality*.[13] It studies what it means to understand the Christian moral life as an integral part of the confessing life of faith.

It follows that personal and social disorientation is caused by the alienation of the divine–human relationship. By, that is, the loss of the sense of the divine presence in human affairs. That loss, according to Christian tradition, is never brought about by a failure on the part of God, it is always the result of human failure. More explicitly, it is brought about by human sinfulness; the self-inflicted alienation of individuals from their Creator. Because they, invariably, do this collectively some Christian liturgical traditions give a central place to the general, that is, collective, confession of sin.

Another theological reason for the central place given to social thinking in Christian theology is the mainstream view it takes of the unity of the body and the soul. Humans are created, according to the biblical image, in a unity of body and spirit. Fidelity to this view caused subsequent generations of Christians to reject all Gnostic and dualistic claims that the body is evil and that it must be rejected if the spirit is to flourish. St Paul used 'the body' as a powerful metaphor to describe how individual Christians should relate to one another. This, in turn, is why Christianity has always put such a high value on *koinonia* (fellowship). This stresses the importance of social relationships sustained by fellowship. At the centre of this fellowship is the sacramental communion of believers with each other and with God.

All this illustrates that Christianity is social and political because of the nature of its doctrine of God. Asocial and apolitical interpretations of Christianity are an aberration, rather than some pure form of it. The same conclusions about the social and political nature of Christianity could also be arrived at in other theological ways. For example, through the Christian doctrine of creation which emphasizes the need for the redemption of all created things, society and politics included.

So far we have seen only that Christianity *is* a social and political religion. We now need to consider in more detail *how* it is so. Some Christians claim that social and political insights follow directly from theological ones and thereby derive their authority from them. However, they have been heavily criticized for doing little or nothing more than baptizing the social and political values of bourgeois liberalism.[14] That may well be true of the way some Christian communities often express themselves, since Christians, like others, are invariably carried along by the political cut and thrust of the societies in which they live. In the midst of all this, however, they are also capable, like others, of making genuine and substantial political contributions to them. Christians, in fact, represent significant opinion-forming bodies, especially in constitutional democracies. Indeed, the extent of that significance may well be out of all proportion to their actual numbers. Little is, in fact, known about the real effect of religion as an influence on public opinion. Wily local politicians, especially if they possess slender majorities, are prudent to cultivate religious interests. The same is true on the larger canvas of national political opinion-forming. In the United States pressure groups and campaigns run by Christian bodies are extremely powerful and in the United Kingdom major church debates and pronouncements on political issues are often dutifully noted by political parties as they seek to display their respect for religiously influenced public opinion. Politicians and others who come in for adverse Christian criticism, as a result, can often be heard to comment that 'the Church should mind its own spiritual business'. Quite apart from this being mistaken for the theological reasons we have given, it makes no sense. Churches like any other public institution cannot be apolitical in this way. Not to speak about such issues is effectively to be just as political as it is to do so.

The question remains, however, does Christianity contain a political agenda? And if it does, can we discover what it is? Such political preferences and attitudes which are expressed in the New Testament, and they are remarkably few, reflect as we should expect the socio-political circumstances which prevailed in first-century Palestine. They show, that is, the exclusion of Christians from political life and in one instance at least Jesus refused to be drawn into controversy about it (Mark 12.17). Little wonder that there are few clues here to help us with our latter-day political and social questions. Indeed, it has been cogently and often argued that Christianity contains no particular political agenda at all and that it is a sacramental religion of spiritual union with God. This criticism would accept the things said above about the relational nature of Christian spirituality, but not accept that it is easy to move from that to a political agenda *per se*. What it argues is that once Christians have established their spirituality, they must turn elsewhere for their political agendas.[15] In direct contrast to this, other Christians claim that Christianity does have an implicit and timeless political agenda, and that it can be derived from the principles of love and justice and in a general 'bias for the poor' which those principles enjoin.[16] Christian Socialism of the late nineteenth and twentieth centuries as found in the writings of Maurice, Tawney and Temple is another example of the view that political principles can be derived from spiritual ones. Indeed, there is something of a significant consensus of scholarly opinion, in the United Kingdom at least, which would locate Christian political and economic values to the left of the political centre.[17] Not even this, however, settles anything in particular, for the simple and obvious reason that Christians on the political right are equally strident in their claims that their agenda is also derived from their spirituality. This is certainly the case in North America where many Christians have been identified with the 'new right' in politics and with its claims to the virtues of the 'free market' and its requirement to lessen the intervention of the state in all levels of economic and political life. In the United Kingdom this is also the political creed of the right and similarly it finds support among some Christians. Clearly, Christianity and politics manifest themselves in diverse ways. All that can surely be required of Christians in politics, whether they speak as individuals or collectively, is that they have some explanation about why they hold the views they do. What must always be avoided, however, is any translation of spiritual into political arrogance which gives rise to dogmatic certainty. This side of the Kingdom of God, all human strivings are less than perfect and perhaps, in the end, that is one of the real insights that Christianity brings to politics.

In the ongoing debate about the nature of Christian engagement with political issues three separate issues recur which are of relevance to pastoral theology. They are the distinction between private and public morality, political realism, and the styles of engagement which Christians use with political issues. We will consider them in turn.

Private and public morality

The distinction between private and public morality is visible whenever it is necessary for individuals to behave in one way when they act on their own behalf and in another when they act on behalf of others. For example, a friend who is a bank manager may be approachable, considerate, kind and generous to a fault – as a friend – ever ready to lend her or his own money to others in need. But in the official capacity of a bank manager this genial friend can become, and indeed must become, a different person: cautious, prudent, able to refuse requests for help and even seemingly disregarding of genuine pleas for assistance. Why is this? It could be because she or he simply chooses to lead a life of double standards, but that is not the point. The point, rather, is that in the official capacity he or she is *obliged* to behave as they do and is not free to choose to do otherwise for the simple reason that the manager is acting on behalf of others and is not lending his or her own money. That obligation is dictated by the policy of the bank and its shareholders as well as by all manner of public and statutory regulation about the lending of money. The manager is also obliged to make a profit out of the loans he or she approves, without which the bank would cease to exist. Note here the extent of the political considerations which managers have to make in discharging this duty. They have a contract with others, the owners of the money. Note too, how the political considerations contrast totally with the unfettered freedom to act which the same persons have in a private capacity when dealing with their own money. The very fact that the two roles are so unlike illustrates that there is a difference in kind between them.

Considerations such as these are unavoidable whenever it is thought necessary to take or allow the taking of lives in pursuit of a just end. The point to note is that considerations about the welfare of groups are different from those about the welfare of individuals. Among other things, they require the taking of a wider and longer view of the issues at stake and, as we have seen, raise issues about justice which seldom feature in matters of private morality. In the latter the highest moral aspiration has to be that of selflessness and self-sacrifice, whereas in social morality the highest aspiration has to be that of justice. A justice which includes wider and longer-term considerations may have to override the immediate interests of individuals. Whereas relationships between individuals can be immediate and spontaneous, those between groups are seldom so, in spite of the lengths they sometimes go to create the impression that they are. Summitry between nations is a good example of this. Those with successful outcomes are invariably preceded by prolonged detailed and tough negotiations in which the results are essentially agreed by skilled negotiators. All this is necessary because groups cannot divest themselves of their power, democratic ones no less than others. Such power is what binds them together. It is, moreover, what gets in the way when they try to deal with each other. It is also the reason why the ethical aspirations of groups have to be shared differently from the way individuals could share them. For example, whereas in individual morality appeals to conscience can be immediate and have dramatic effects, this is not possible between groups because there is no collective parallel facility.

Groups are held together by all manner of coercion, acceptable or otherwise, and this, again, causes them to be ever-mindful of their self-interest. Indeed, inter-group negotiations are invariably at their most successful when balances of self-interest can be maintained. Whatever is agreed has to have something in it for everybody. Some will see this as cynicism and counter the argument by claiming that groups will never behave ethically unless they yield to individual criticism and example. For such, the distinction between two moralities is unacceptable. Moreover it is often cited as a cause of public immorality and claimed that this can only be overcome if individual moral values are projected without qualification into the public arena. So many disagreements about morality turn on this very point. They often feature protagonists who on the one hand assert that their private moralities, whatever they might be, are the sole guiding principle of their public ones and those on the other who want to point out that there are other considerations at stake. Sometimes this polarity is modified with the result that the difference between the two positions is less clear. Examples of this can often be found in debates between pacifists and non-pacifists, whenever any of the former show that they are prepared to take wider pragmatic considerations into account. Indeed it is largely because of considerations such as these that pacifism, for example, exists in so many different forms.

Acceptance of the view that there is a difference between private and public morality does not, of course, rule out discussion of the possibility that each might influence the other. This is, in fact, invariably what does happen in debates about morality. Those concerning the acceptability or otherwise of abortion are a case in point. But the two views of morality cannot be easily reconciled and, perhaps, ought not to be. In his classic discussion of the topic Reinhold Niebuhr writes, 'It would therefore seem better to accept a frank dualism in morals than to attempt a harmony between the two methods which threatens the effectiveness of both.'[18]

Advocates of the distinction between the two moralities often make appeal to the need for the consideration of political realism in moral debate. By this they mean that moral opinions must, of necessity, be translatable into politically realistic solutions. Brief consideration of the nature of political realism will illustrate this claim and we will follow that with further consideration of one way in which aspects of the distinction between the two moralities has borne upon related debates about how churches should pronounce on complex issues of social morality.

Political realism

Not surprisingly, the theologian who influentially outlined the difference between the two moralities also, as a consequence, wrote on the subject of political realism. Reinhold Niebuhr, was, as we have seen, a third-generation American theologian of European origin. He agreed with Karl Barth that the notion of dialectic was central to the understanding of the divine–human encounter. Whereas for Barth, however, that dialectic was understood as operating between God and the Church, hence the title of his *magnum opus*, *Church Dogmatics*, for Niebuhr the dialectic was between God's righteousness and all human activity. His insights into this arose from his work as a pastor in Detroit. There he tried to discern the significance of the word of God for the actual circumstances of the lives of thousands of people who worked on the mass production of motor vehicles. The processes used, Niebuhr observed, seemed to deny the humanity of those who were engaged in them. This denial, he believed, was most manifest in the complacency with which all involved in the processes accepted the tenets of the materialism of which they were a part. Niebuhr's problem, as a pastor, focused on the realization that preaching 'spiritual ideals' to such people was an irrelevance, since they had their own set of ideals, all of which had to do more with the acquisition of present material values than with the contemplation of eternal spiritual ones. Because of this, he enquired whether there might be some form of spiritual idealism which would be realistic enough to say something about the inherent and radical exploitation of labour and class conflict which was a common feature of the production processes.

Niebuhr was not the first to address himself to such questions in North America. They had featured prominently in the work of the nineteenth-century 'social gospel' of Rauschenbusch and others. What distinguished Niebuhr's approach from them was that he did not write, in the first instance at least, academic theology for its own sake. He wrote in strident prose on a number of issues in publicly accessible journals and newspapers. He refused, in so doing, to neglect any aspects of the situations he addressed, however ugly and repulsive they might appear to have been. In this way, Niebuhr began his subsequently distinguished career in secular political involvements. He wrote on issues as diverse as race relations and labour rates. As a result, his theology was developed in close relation to present political, economic and social events and it commanded the attention of those concerned with them, thereby fulfilling the earlier requirement to discover a dialectic between the word of God and all human affairs. To this he gave the name of 'Christian realism', since it is created out of a combination of empirical pragmatism and a refusal to ignore 'the universality of man's tendency to egocentricity'.[19]

Niebuhr had a self-declared lack of interest in theories of knowledge or philosophy for its own sake, so wrote comparatively little on Christian realism as an abstract concept. Instead, he wrote copiously on the relevance of the Christian faith to political issues understood in this way. In so doing, he sought to make the word of God relevant to secular life. This should not be mistaken for a self-defeating relativism. On the one hand, for Niebuhr, there were absolute norms of conduct and value and, on the other, he recognized that these can never be fully realized this side of the Kingdom of God. In any instance absolute values, such as love and justice, are only approximated. There are many reasons for this and chief among them, as we have seen, is human sinfulness which ensures that even the very best of human endeavour is imperfect in the sight of God and will remain so this side of his Kingdom. Moreover, we have to live with the fact that the requirements of love and justice can seemingly conflict with each other, but not allow this to prevent us from trying to reconcile and realize their ideals in any given situation. For this reason, according to Niebuhr, it is not possible to work out an *a priori* theory of Christian political realism. Neat and universally binding deductions cannot be derived from lofty ideals. The alternative was to accept a pragmatism made necessary by contingencies as they presented themselves. Theological contributions to political debate therefore had to relate to actual circumstances and be specific even if, of necessity, they were also imperfect and incomplete.

The attractions of this position are obvious. From a theological point of view it is profoundly incarnational since it takes the actual circumstances of the created order seriously. It also refuses to romanticize the notion of creation by ignoring its uglier aspects as has so often been the case in Christian writing on the subject. A recent example can be found in the criticisms made by R. H. Preston and C. Birch of the World Council of Churches' use of the phrase 'the integrity of creation'. The WCC, they argue, has allowed ideology to prevail over scientifically-based common sense. As a result, they claim, the theological conclusions drawn by the WCC are erroneous. In the spirit of political realism, they urge the WCC to look at the created order as it actually is and then seek its transformation in the sight of God.[20] All such political realism is an implicit rejection of any sort of dualism in human affairs. It holds that no area of life and thought can remain impervious to the redeeming grace of God. Neat and separate categories of the spiritual and the secular are rejected, in favour of a vision which sees all creation yielding to God's redeeming grace. This accepts that the Kingdom of God cannot be established on earth by dint of human effort. Its inauguration is in God's gift alone. It lies in some presently unknown future. In the meantime, that Kingdom is, by grace, partially reflected in human affairs, thereby redeeming them and raising them to otherwise unattainable levels of perfection, however imperfect in a greater vision they might be and remain. All this imposes a provisionality on Christian 'solutions' to political problems which the religious temperament, often preferring certainties, frequently finds uncongenial. It reminds us that

Christian solutions to political and economic problems are no more or no less certain than secular ones. This is why pedantic certainty can so easily become the antithesis of political responsibility. The reason for this is that Niebuhr, and others, have denied that such certainties can be derived from any religious or other premises which are independent of political, economic and other empirical concerns. There are no such premises from which inerrant principles can be deduced. Note that this insight can equally be applied to systems of secular political theory. Whenever fidelity to such systems is demanded in a way which ignores empirical facts, then we do well to remember the insights of political realism.

One more thing needs to be noted about political realism. It often creates an entrée into political action in the sense that it makes political power structures accessible to those with ideals. Utopians of all kinds who refuse to take the actual circumstances of given political situations seriously are seldom entrusted, if at all, or at least not for long, with political power. A good example is the way in the United Kingdom in which the new Labour Party in opposition and in government has been reviewing its commitment to older dogmatically held policies. As a result, it achieved a large parliamentary majority in a comparatively short space of time simply by making itself electable to those who previously mistrusted its dogmas such as unilateral nuclear disarmament and the public ownership of utilities. Indeed, such realism is also a common feature of contemporary international politics with the collapse of the former Soviet system being the most dramatic example. Unqualified utopianism is also giving way to politically acceptable realism in the fragile areas of international peacemaking.

Middle axioms

Even if the above claims about political and Christian realism are acceptable, they still leave open questions about how Christian political engagement with political processes should occur. It will, of course, do so in many ways and primary among them will be through the labours of individual Christians working within established political structures alongside those of other faiths and beliefs.

Most of the major Christian denominations have Boards or other agencies which exist for the purpose of clarifying Christian opinion on moral and political issues. In addition, the World Council of Churches sustains its own commentary on them. In sum, all this marks a very real attempt to establish responsible Christian living amid perplexity. But is raises recurrent and common difficulties. To what extent, for example, should such clarification go into technical complexity? Should it, rather, simply note it and produce general guidelines to inform conduct? Or should it try to make detailed and specific recommendations on all manner of pastoral issues? How, in other words, should the balance be struck between vague generality and detailed prescriptivism? General statements are likely to secure the most support because they allow for a variety of interpretation. The more specific any recommendations become the more likely they are to generate disagreement. It is easy to criticize both of these approaches. Against generality it can be asked, how can it ever be specific enough to influence actual policy decisions? And against specificity it can be held that the likelihood of error increases as the nature of the specifics become debatable. Is there a way of solving such dilemmas?

One influential attempt to claim that there is was first mentioned by J. H. Oldham and W. A. Visser 't Hooft in *The Church and its Function in Society*, published in 1937. They claimed that broad assertions 'do not go far toward helping the individual to know what he ought to do in particular cases'.[21] To counter this, however, with only detailed recommendations is equally unsatisfactory, 'it is not the function of the clergy to tell the laity how to act in public affairs'.[22] Their preferred solution was for the Church to confront people with what they called the 'Christian demand' and to let them work out for themselves what it might mean or require in any instance. 'Hence between purely general statements of the ethical demands of the Gospel and the decisions that have to be made in concrete situations there is need for what may be called "middle axioms".'[23] These are described as

> An attempt to define the directions in which, in a particular state of society, Christian faith must express itself. They are not binding for all time, but are provisional definitions of the type of behaviour required of Christians at a given period and in given circumstances.[24]

To say, therefore, that a maxim is 'middle' is to say of it that it is located between generality of the one hand and specificity of the other.

In a subsequent defence of middle axioms, Ronald Preston claims that they are 'arrived at by bringing alongside one another the total Christian understanding of life and an analysis of the empirical situation'. The result is a 'halfway stage between what is clear Christian judgement and what is an opinion subject to empirical hazards and checks'.[25] Preston goes on to claim that such axioms have a high informal authority, but he is clear on the fact that 'they do not go as far as policy formulation'.[26] For this reason, he concludes that the obligation to create such formulation is left to individuals and groups who alone can work out what any axiom might require in given circumstances. Does this approach still help with understanding how pastorally effective decisions can be made in complex societies which are dominated by ever increasing technological innovation? Brief consideration of the debates about modern warfare will illustrate this question.

In 1930 the Lambeth Conference of Anglican Bishops endorsed the following statement on war: 'the Christian must condemn war not merely because it is wasteful and ruinous, a cause of untold misery, but far more because it is contrary to the will of God'.[27] This statement was also endorsed by the Bishops at subsequent Lambeth Conferences. It contradicted, without explanation, the centuries-old and continuing Christian view there can be wars which are thought to be just, by saying that Christians have nothing to say about war apart from the fact that it should never be undertaken. This statement has many of the hallmarks of a 'middle axiom'. It is clear without being specific and aspires to what Preston calls 'high informal authority'. Its clear weakness is that it is over-prescriptive to the point of prohibiting all war.

What, it must be asked, was the relevance of the statement to the situation Britain confronted in 1939? It was of no help to those – many of whom had formerly been pacifists, such as Bertrand Russell[28] – who believed that the evils of Nazism had to be militarily resisted. Against the policy direction indicated by the statement, many then held, and still do, that war can be used reluctantly as an instrument of acceptable policy providing that it is waged according to strict controlling criteria. The Lambeth statement was less than helpful in 1939 to any but those who were pacifists. For the guidance of the majority of Christians there was need for something which was equally authoritative but much less prescriptive. The Lambeth statement does not, of course, meet the requirements of middle axiom theory, since it is far too prescriptive in one direction. Some such statement as 'war is to be avoided wherever possible and only engaged in according to strict criteria (whatever they may be)' would have been equally authoritative and more enabling to those who struggled with their consciences in the dark hours of 1939.

The struggle still prevails. Indeed, in the nuclear age it is more pressing than ever. Whether or not the deployment of nuclear weapons as deterrents to war, or whether or not the limited use of some types of nuclear weapons could be morally acceptable, has been the subject of extensive recent moral debate, not a little of which has been generated by those reflecting on the issues from a Christian point of view.[29] In what sense, it must be asked, do middle axioms actually help in this debate? What they enjoin may be laudable, but do they actually help with making difficult policy decisions? On the prospect of nuclear war, there will always be those on the one hand who believe it to be so radically evil that it should never be contemplated, as there will also be those on the other who claim that in some form nuclear deterrence and even nuclear war fighting might be the lesser of possible evils. In all this, difficult policy decisions have to be taken and, possibly, radical evils denounced. This issue is discussed by Paul Ramsey in *Who Speaks for the Churches?*, in response to a criticism of middle axiom theory made by Ralph Potter who argued that certain evils should be radically and unequivocally denounced in ways that left no room for any so called middle ground. He writes, 'I take it that at some point, perhaps at the gateway of Auschwitz, the Christian should speak very specifically against the outrageous crimes of his government. How does he decide when that time has come?'[30] Ramsey put forward two observations in reply to Potter. First, that Auschwitz was an exception (would that this were true), and that to say nothing until the gates are reached may well be too late. And second, that saying no to outrageous crime is not to be confused with the evaluation of complex policy options. Ramsey was not an advocate of middle axioms. His preference was for what he called 'action and decision oriented principles'. Principles, that is, that can be more prescriptive than middle axiom theory would permit. His difference with Potter, however, well illustrates the central difficulty with middle axiom theory in that it calls attention to its weakness in the face of radical evil, as well as to its at least potential vacuity in the face of the need to make hard policy decisions. Other critical considerations also need to be made of the theory.

Whereas we saw earlier that the concept of 'political realism' opened an understanding of there being a dialectic between spiritual insights and specific circumstances, middle axiom theory appears, at least, to restrict reference to the latter. This being so, it seems to prevent Christian insight from becoming incarnational in the sense of enabling it to transform the actual circumstances of life, particularly when they threaten its well-being and even very existence. Although defenders of the theory may well reply that individuals or groups should effect such incarnational engagement, it remains to be asked in what precise way the theory enables them to do so? Helpful and necessary though it may well be for attention to be drawn to general principles, something more specific is invariably needed in dire situations such as those concerning modern warfare. Hard choices are unavoidable.

A further difficulty with middle axiom theory arises from its view of technical expertise. Actual policy decisions are invariably made in the light of highly technical and ever-changing information which only experts, and maybe only a few of them at that, can master. Others can only trust them to act in the best interest of all and can do nothing to assist beyond calling the attention of the experts to the guiding potential of middle axioms. But can experts be trusted in this way? And does their expertise alone justify us in hoping that they can be? There are clearly areas of life where it must be right to trust experts in this way, but they are invariably ones in which we have some other and good reason for doing so. Examples of this occur whenever we know that such experts are governed by enforceable codes of conduct and/or legislation. Indeed the not uncommon call for such occurs whenever it is suspected that experts are acting autonomously on behalf of others beyond the reach of accountability or control of any kind. The attitude to expertise which is embedded in middle axiom theory is noticeably deferential and clearly predates the contemporary and widespread insistence on calling such expertise to account. An insistence which has no doubt arisen, in large measure, from the recent, tragic and repeated experiences of the fallibility of expertise. To say this is not to denigrate at all either the importance or the value of expertise. It is but to caution against expecting it to deliver more than it is capable of when total human well-being is at stake. Its fallibility derives from the fallibility of the human beings who deploy it. No expertise can be free of this. Clearly, technical expertise is relevant to moral decision making, but it is only a part of it. Decisions which affect whole societies require wider participation. For this reason alone, middle axiom theory has its limitations.

The processes whereby the redemption of social structures is effected remains a complex one. This chapter has simply pointed out that it requires considerations which are different from those which are required for understanding the redemption of individuals. It is imperative that the peoples of the world agree to live together in peace in ways which respect and preserve the natural environment and bring justice to bear on the equity with which its finite resources are distributed. Pastoral theologies must be deemed inadequate unless they are capable of both recognizing and making a contribution to this, in considerable detail when necessary. This is why, as we have seen throughout, pastoral theology is pervaded with moral issues, to a consideration of which we now turn.

Notes

1   For an excellent recent discussion about the care of individuals in situations of social conflict see Couture, P. D. and Hunter, R. J. (1995) *Pastoral Care and Social Conflict*, Nashville: Abingdon.
2   See Preston, R. H. (1981) *Explorations in Theology, 9*, London: SCM.
3   Neibuhr, Reinhold (1932) *Moral Man and Immoral Society*, pp. 74 ff. New York: Scribners.
4   See pp. 12–13, this volume.
5   Bonhoeffer, D. (1955) *Ethics*, pp. 179–84. London: SCM.
6   Schmitt, C. (1970) *Politische Theologie*, Berlin: Duncker and Humbolt.
7   Metz, J. B. (1969) *Theology of the World*, New York: Herder; London: Search.
8   Sollë, D., trans. Shelley, John (1974) *Political Theology*, Philadelphia: Fortress.
9   Moltmann, Jürgen with Meeks, M. Douglas (25 December 1978) 'The liberation of oppressors'. *Christianity and Crisis*, 310–17.
10   See Cobb, John B. (Jr.) (1982) *Process Theology as Political Theology*, pp. 1–18. Manchester: Manchester University Press.
11   Preston, *Explorations in Theology, 9*, p. 93.
12   Ibid.
13   Forrester, Duncan (1997) *The True Church and Morality*, Geneva: WCC. See also Mudge, L. S. (1998) *The Church as Moral Community*, New York: Continuum.
14   See Norman, E. (1979) *Christianity and the World Order*, Oxford: Oxford University Press.
15   Powell, E. (1977) *Wrestling with the Angel*, pp. 43–4. London: Sheldon.
16   Hiltner, S. (1949) *Pastoral Counselling*, p. 19. New York: Abingdon.
17   See Preston, R. H. (1983) *Church and Society in the Late Twentieth Century: the Economic and Political Task*, London: SCM.
18   Niebuhr, Reinhold (1932) *Moral Man and Immoral Society*, pp. 270–1. New York: Scribners.
19   Niebuhr, Reinhold (1953) *Christian Realism and Political Problems*, p. 17. London: Faber & Faber.
20   Cf. Preston, R. H. and Birch, C. (1998) *Facts and Fables in Ecology and the Integrity of Creation*, Liverpool: Liverpool Hope University College Press.
21   Oldham, J. H. and Visser 't Hooft, W. A. (1937) *The Church and its Function in Society*, p. 209. London: George Allen & Unwin.
22   Ibid., p. 209.
23   Ibid., pp. 209–10.
24   Ibid., p. 210.
25   Preston, *Explorations in Theology, 9*, pp. 39–40.
26   Ibid.
27   *The Lambeth Conference*, 1930, London: SPCK.
28   Russell, B. (1968) *The Autobiography of Bertrand Russell, Vol. 2*, p. 191. London: George Allen & Unwin.

29   Cf. Bauckham, R. J. and Elford, R. J. (1989) *The Nuclear Weapons Debate*, London: SCM.
30   Ramsey, P. (1969) *Who Speaks for the Churches?*, p. 42. Edinburgh: Saint Andrew Press.

7

Morality and care

The conception of pastoral theology developed in this book is a multi-faceted one. Initially, it focused on the theme of 'care' as found in the biblical traditions and developed in Christian tradition. We have also seen the need for it to be 'in conversation' with contemporary culture and for it to embrace the social as well as the individual dimensions of human welfare. This final chapter will look at morality in the context of pastoral theology. It will show that, although the purview of pastoral theology is broader than morality, moral issues are an inextricable part of all pastoral theology and care. At the end of the chapter we will discuss some contemporary issues of morality which present profound pastoral problems. In this way, we will see how the biblical faith remains in the making when its theology is also made and remade in the light of pastoral need.

For this reason alone, pastors and those interested in the pastoral as we have been discussing it, need to understand how moral problems 'present' themselves, how, that is, we recognize them for what they are. In doing this they need, also, to be aware of how religious and secular influences interact and for that reason the latter will also be discussed in a way which brings out their strengths and weaknesses. For example, we will discuss ethical utilitarianism not only because it is, in the West at least, an all-pervasive influence in morality, but because, from a pastoral point of view, it is widely assumed that individuals and societies prosper best if their actions bring about morally desirable ends. In fact, the desirability of bringing about such ends is not infrequently given as justification for this or that pastoral preference.

Just one common example of this is the way the well-being of children is, rightly, cited as a central concern in discussions about the propriety or otherwise of divorce. We will also consider some of the great themes which Christianity brings to bear on morality and reflect on just how moral issues relate to pastoral ones with reference to particular topics.

The 'faces' of morality

It is helpful to imagine that morality has three faces. These are not always separable from each other and they occur in ever-changing combinations. For this reason 'face' is meant to mean something like 'appearance' or 'manifestation'. It is what we see when we confront a moral problem.

The first face of morality is the 'human' one. Moral problems are experienced uniquely, we might presume, by human beings. They can arise from facts to which, as we shall see, they have a complex and debated relationship, but they are decidedly human because it is only human beings who experience the rational freedom to choose between alternative courses of action. Even though some choices may be illusory, and even if humans are at times unknowingly manipulated to make actual choices, human freedom is the basis of morality. Indeed, freedom of choice, as well as being of the essence of morality itself, is also the essence of what it means to be human. It is a given, or *a priori*, feature of human existence. To exercise such freedom of choice is to be human, and to fail to do so is invariably to deny one's humanity. This is the point where many of the classical explorations and theories of morality begin.[1] It has been suggested that we become aware of moral problems when we encounter conflicts of interest.[2] When, that is, we become aware of the equally competing claims of two or more courses of action. Such conflict can be unbearable, which is why experiencing moral problems, however trivial they might seem to others, can cause considerable personal anguish. The most overwhelming human experience of this kind is the experience of tragedy. The experience, that is, that things could have been other than as they often tragically are, had different choices been made. What is tragic is what was avoidable.[3] All choices, even sometimes the most seemingly trivial ones, can cause conflict, anguish and in extreme cases lead to tragedy. For all these reasons, individuals are sometimes totally debilitated by their inability to make up their minds about moral problems or about decisions that have been made, but which may be subsequently regretted. All this can equally apply to groups as to individuals. Deep divisions of interest can be as destructive of societies as they can be of individuals. In these ways morality touches the very stuff of what it means to be human.

The pastoral significance of understanding morality in this way as a protean feature of human freedom is obvious. For many individuals, such freedom is too much to bear and they crave to be given direction by others, hoping that powers not their own will make for righteousness. This is what makes authoritarian systems of morality so attractive to many, especially when they are accompanied by paternalistic claims that the authority is exercised in the individual's best interest. When, that is, the external moral authority is seen to be earnest in its pastoral endeavour. Some religious moralities are obviously of this kind. Before we consider this further, it is necessary to consider the other two faces of morality.

The second is what we may call the 'factual' face of morality, so-called because all moral problems invariably contain reference to factual information, some of which is extremely complex. Furthermore, it may not be obvious which facts are relevant to a particular moral problem and which are not. Indeed, it has traditionally been claimed that none of them can be, since there is a logical gap between facts and values and that to suppose otherwise is to commit the so-called 'naturalistic fallacy'. This was famously championed by the Scottish empiricist philosopher David Hume (d. 1776) and taken up afresh by G. E. Moore at the beginning of the twentieth century.[4] According to this view, it is mistaken to suppose that values can be derived from facts, on the ground that values are independent from facts which are, in themselves, value-free. This is, moreover, a somewhat popular view of the nature of the relationship of facts to values. It holds that we live in a world of facts on the one hand and of values on the other. We can bring values to bear on facts, but we cannot derive values from them.

In mid-twentieth-century moral philosophy this view was examined in what has been called the 'Is–Ought Debate'. In this the older and early-twentieth-century view of the separateness of facts and values has been increasingly challenged. It has been argued, for example, that facts are so inextricably entwined with moral problems that they must be seen as a part of them, even a logical part. Whereas the technical detail of this contemporary version of the debate need not detain us, we cannot overlook its importance, especially in an age when so many of our moral problems relate to, or arise from, complex facts, many of which have to do with our ever-emerging new technologies. One suggested way of dealing with the question about identifying those facts which do relate to moral problems and those which do not, is to distinguish between facts which are 'brute' facts, in the sense that they have no obvious relation to particular moral problems, and 'institutional' facts, which do so relate.[5] These are facts, such as those arising from technologies which we have mentioned, a specific example of which would be *in vitro* fertilization. This is in one sense a 'brute' fact but it is more than that, it is relative (to say the least), to questions about the morality or otherwise of issues concerning human reproductivity. Numerous other such clear examples could be given of facts which are at the centre of current debates about morality.

Suppose, then, that without seeking any final word in this largely unsolved philosophical debate, we accept that some facts are 'relative' to moral problems; what then follows? First, we have to establish ways of finding out which facts are relative in this way and which are not. This is, invariably, a more difficult thing to do than it may appear, since our view of the facts at issue is often coloured by our preconceived moral opinions. A well-known example of this is found in the debate about nuclear weapons, and in particular about the efficacy of their deployment as deterrents. Supporters of such deployment have often claimed that the weapons have 'kept the peace for forty years', and opponents of the view contest that claim, even suggesting that the weapons, so deployed, have caused or at least contributed to the unsatisfactory nature of what their proponents call 'peace'. This example alone shows that there are no such things as 'value-free' facts. The emotive way in which we often refer to them confirms the point. Clearly, progress with this problem must be made if, in an increasingly factually complex society, we are to conduct such debates in a rational and morally beneficial way. But, as long as so much of our moral confusion arises from areas where we are ever pushing our technologies to their limits, it is unlikely that all factual confusions and disputes will be eliminated entirely from moral debates.

So, getting facts straight is more difficult than at first sight it seems to be. Although much more could be said about the 'factual' face of morality, we have said enough to recognize it and to see that treating it as a 'face' of morality enables us to understand a little better just one of the three main ways in which moral problems present themselves.

The third face of morality is the 'analytic' one. This shows that moral problems are susceptible of analysis because we can discern methods, patterns and principles in moral decision making. These, in themselves, do little to solve moral problems, but they are the means whereby the nature of morality is subjected to rational analysis.

The most common form of analysis is philosophical analysis. Some have argued that this analysis of morality is a 'second order' discipline, in the sense that it is carried out by observers of, rather than by participants in, moral debates.[6] Such an observer, it is argued, would not be concerned about the acceptability, or otherwise, of the actual moral conclusions which are arrived at. She or he would, rather, simply analyse the *means* whereby they are arrived at. This is what is meant by calling it a 'second order' activity, in relation to the 'first order' activity of those who actually make moral decisions, often without attempting any such 'second order' analysis of them. In its strongest form, this 'second order' view of the nature of moral analysis even stresses that it is necessary for the analyst not to be involved in 'first order' debate at all, since if they were it might compromise the degree of objectivity which the 'second order' analysis requires. This is why so-called 'second order' analysts have even made it something of a virtue to eschew interest in actual moral decisions. Their aim is to produce analyses of such clarity and relevance that they will, in turn, enable 'first order' participants in moral decision making to have a clearer understanding of what they are doing and thereby make more informed, or better, moral decisions than they would without the benefit of such analysis. But, is this an acceptable account of what the analysis of moral problems should be like? There is obviously much to be said for the dispassionate analysis of moral problems, especially where they are compounded by highly emotive feelings. The value of this must not be overlooked. Note, however, that the value of such analysis is only realized if it is taken note of by someone else, namely, the participants in moral decision making. The philosophical analyst here offers something for consideration and seemingly does not press unduly for its acceptance. To do that would be to take part in 'first order' debate. It is here that the 'first' and 'second' order distinction between morality and its analysis begins to break down. It does so because the degree of objectivity it requires of the analyst, whilst laudable, is unrealizable. The degree of detachment it requires of human beings is too great. Machines like computers can process and analyse factual information and, if we can programme them adequately for the purpose, they can do so either without bias, or at least with bias we can observe and allow for. Human beings are not like this, especially when they study moral issues. They are affected, whether they are aware of it or not, by dint of their humanity. Maintaining the detached pose at all times, therefore, requires an unattainable degree of disinterested objectivity. Unless analysing moral problems is like doing a crossword (that is, for its own sake) then its engagement with actual moral decision making cannot be ignored. Recognizing this does not mean, of course, that we should not strive for such objectivity in moral debate as can be achieved. Thus we may conclude that the recently popular belief that the philosophical analysis of moral problems is a 'second order' activity needs to be treated with caution, in favour of a view which sees such analysis as an integral part of the moral decision making process itself.

Throughout this discussion we have referred to the task of seeking solutions to moral problems. But, what actually are these solutions? Answers to this question usually vary according to particular understandings of the nature of morality. For example, if we believe that 'goodness' has some objective quality, then a solution to a moral problem could be said to be found whenever we identify its presence, in the sense that we would also know how to recognize its absence. Yet again, if, as we shall see, goodness is thought to be something that attaches to the desirability of the consequences of our actions, then moral problems are 'solved' when that desirability is realized, or at least when it has the prospect of being so. There is, in fact, no single definition of moral goodness which commands enough support for it to stand as a universal norm. Sometimes in the past, there may or may not have been actual widespread agreement about what constitutes moral goodness, but it is not the case today for reasons which have to do with the complex plurality of Western culture. This reaches back certainly to the break-up of the mediaeval synthesis between religion and philosophy in the Renaissance. Ever since that time, diverse interests have been at work and they have had the effect of producing different outlooks on religious belief and secular ideology. All this has given rise to the existence of different approaches to morality. Simple overviews of the nature of goodness are for this reason no longer available to us. They may exist by agreement among groups of religious believers or secular ideologues, but they do not prevail among those outside such groups. The majority of us now live with the knowledge of several theories about what moral goodness is, and many of these compete with, and even contradict each other. Attempts to press the exclusive superiority of one theory over others are now comparatively uncommon. What most people, in fact, do is to strive for moral insight by drawing on a number of different theories and traditions. I will now discuss some of the key concepts and debates which feature in this, starting with two overtly biblical notions: love and justice. Following that, we will examine a variety of more secular concepts which will include intrinsic moral values, utilitarianism and natural law. I shall show that pastoral theology cannot afford to identify exclusively, or even too strictly, with any particular concept of the moral life, if the mysteries which attach to each are to be respected.

Love

From the point of view of Christian pastoral theology the first account of moral goodness that comes to mind is that of love. Not love in general, but the love of God in Jesus which is referred to in the New Testament and throughout subsequent Christian history as *agape*. This is the unstinting love of God for creation. It is virtually un-self-regarding and seeks only the total well-being of its object. The only knowledge we have of it is in the ministry of Jesus. 'I give you a new commandment, that you love one another. Just as I have loved you, you should also love one another' (John 13.34). The centrality of love in the Christian life is emphasized, even first established on anything like a systematic basis, by St Paul who was also preoccupied with exploring what it required (e.g., 1 Cor 13). St Paul, however, never quotes the words of Jesus, so we naturally get no mention of what he (Jesus) said about love. The practice of Christian love became the hallmark of Christian community life as it was, for example, in the communities which produced the Johannine writings of the New Testament. In the early centuries, Christian writers repeatedly explored the nature and significance of love in the Christian life, this culminating in the writings of St Augustine whose systematic theology centres on the love of humankind to God. Augustine distinguished *eros* (human love) from *agape* (divine love) and sought to relate the two. This he did by pointing out the limitations of human love. It could reach only so far out to God but no further. This limitation is caused by its very nature, which Augustine called *superbia.* This arises out of the self-sufficiency and pride of human love.

According to Augustine, the relation between *agape* and *eros* is therefore as follows. *Eros*, left to itself, can see God and feel itself drawn to him. But it sees God only at a remote distance; between him and the soul lies an immense ocean, and when the soul imagines it has reached him it has simply entered, in self-sufficiency and pride, into the harbour of itself. But for pride, *eros* would be able to bring the soul to God. Here *agape* must come to its assistance: God's *humilitas* must vanquish man's *superbia*. For even if all other ties that bind the soul to things earthly and transient are broken, its ascent will not succeed so long as it is infected with *superbia*. By *superbia* the soul is chained to itself and cannot ascend to what is above itself. It is the task of *agape* to sever this last link of the soul with things finite.[7]

In this way human love is carried upwards to God, its self-limitation no longer in operation. Augustine called the point where the limitation of human love was freed by divine love *caritas*, which is a fusion by *agape* of itself with human love. St Augustine, as we have seen, further claimed that these two loves existed in two 'cities', the earthly and the heavenly. In this way Augustine not only produced a theology of Christian love which could explain the sudden loss of confidence in *eros* brought about by the fall of Rome in 410 CE, he also laid the theological foundations for the understanding of the nature of love in Western Christianity.

To seek the good from a Christian point of view is, therefore, in large part at least, to seek love. But how do we know what love actually requires of us when we face specific moral problems? For example, it would be easy to elicit from a group of Christians agreement that they should order their lives around the principle of love so understood. Suppose, for instance, that such a group was shipwrecked and wanted to observe love as a basis for life of unknown duration on a desert island. With such an agreement they could reasonably set about that life with some confidence. But, inevitably, specific moral problems would soon present themselves, thrown up by the everyday business of ordinary life. How was labour to be divided? How were finite resources to be distributed among those who had seemingly equal but different claims to them? Whose opinion would prevail if different and contentious opinions arose over plans for escape? And so on. No area of life is immune for long, if at all, from such questions. Prior agreement that the loving thing should always be done would not, however earnestly and sincerely it had been entered into, in itself ensure agreement about answers to specific questions. Disagreement would inevitably occur. Moreover, the disagreeing parties would all, in view of the prior commitment to do the loving thing, be expected to claim that their answers to the questions were required by love. As a result, disagreements in the name of love would then prevail, just as they have actually done throughout Christian history. The reason for this is plainly because love in itself is not an unequivocal guide to moral action. In spite of this, love remains central to the Christian pursuit of goodness, but it does not provide an all-sufficient way of finding out what goodness is. Love can, indeed, inspire heroic action and, more, can sustain it to the nth degree. But other considerations such as those of justice will properly always intrude, if love is ever to be more than lofty sentiment.[8] Love thus becomes more not less important in the Christian view of morality when we recognize, rather than ignore, its limitations.

Justice

Justice in Christian theology has been seen as (in the Old Testament) the exercise of compassion and mercy to the poor; as a cardinal virtue along with prudence, temperance, and fortitude; and as a means whereby the requirements of love are distributed equally to all. Such a Christian understanding of justice has been advocated by E. Clinton Gardner in *Justice and Christian Ethics*.[9] This book is an important recent contribution to the contemporary debate about justice which was prompted by the publication of *A Theory of Justice* by John Rawls in 1971. Whereas Rawls advocated the need for justice to focus on the nature of rights and duties in an egalitarian society, with a bias towards the underprivileged, Gardner takes the discussion back to much older Judaeo-Christian views of justice as covenant and virtue. He sees this as the basis of communities in which sin is restrained and democracy preserved or recovered. 'Understood in terms of covenant, justice is perceived fundamentally as promise.'[10] The theological origins of covenant and promise which make this view of justice possible, also enable it to transcend positive law and specific social embodiment, thereby creating the possibility of a pluralism in which reverence for the otherness and even the 'objectivity' of justice makes the pursuit of a common good possible. Gardner sees the secular tasks of justice as 'love's work' and is clear about the fact that it cannot do what is required of it unless it is placed in its older Judaeo-Christian setting.

Intrinsic moral values

Another approach to moral goodness from a Christian point of view claims that there are *intrinsic* rights and wrongs. These admit of no exception whatsoever, totally regardless of any circumstances which might suggest otherwise. Christians have most commonly claimed this about things they suppose to be according to the will of God, as it is revealed in Scripture. A good example is the sixth commandment 'Thou shall not kill.' Many Christians argue that the literal acceptance of this commandment, without exception, is a necessary condition of Christian discipleship, in the sense that a person who claimed to be a Christian but also believed that it was legitimate, even in limited and carefully defined circumstances, to kill, would not be a Christian at all. All killing, on this view, is self-evidently and intrinsically wrong. This is just one example of a range of moral views which can be expressed in this way. What they have in common is the central conviction that they are all intrinsically justified in the sense explained.[11] It should be noted, however, that the obvious harshness of expressing moral values in this way has not been without mitigation. Without at all allowing that intrinsic values can ever be other than as they are, some have sought to mitigate this harshness with forms of casuistic interpretation which give, so to speak, the seeming harshness of intrinsic values a human face. Casuistry is not, therefore, as it is often thought, simply a way of disregarding intrinsic values. It is, rather, a way of preserving them on the one hand and of mitigating their harshness on the other. Examples of such casuistry can be found throughout Judaeo-Christian history. The moral teaching of the Pharisees in the New Testament and that of the Jesuits in the sixteenth century are but two well-known examples. Both of these attracted harsh criticism from rigorists who, mistakenly, believed that that intrinsic rights could never admit of exception.

Understanding moral values to be intrinsically self-justifying has, invariably, led to the further claim that once they are recognized for what they are, it becomes our *duty* to abide by them. This is why this view of morality is often called *deontological*, the study of duty. This word is most commonly taken to mean that acts, so described, are intrinsically right, regardless of any circumstances or consequences which might suggest otherwise. The most influential deontologist in modern times is Immanuel Kant (1724–1804). What he did, among other things, was to put deontology on a formal basis by showing that it was a fundamental part of the ordinary moral experience of every individual. He argued that morality is autonomous in the sense that it does not depend on anything other than itself for either its existence or its explanation. Morality, on this view, is not derived from religion, quite the reverse. Kant argued that morality led *ineluctably* to religion and claimed that Christianity was the most moral of all religions. In *Groundwork of the Metaphysic of Morals* (1785), Kant arrived at this conclusion by way of propositions. The first is that it is 'impossible to conceive anything at all in this world, or even out of it, which can be taken as good without qualification except a good will'.[12] This is because it is only by the exercise of such a will that duty can be done. Values are not good because of what they can achieve or bring about, they are good in themselves. Such a good will is related to duty because an action 'done from duty has its moral worth, not the purpose to be attained by it, but in the maxim in accordance with which it is decided upon'.[13] Objects, or ends, have no place in this sort of thinking, what matters is that duty is an act of conforming the will to its requirements. But what are these requirements? How do we proceed from such a formal definition of duty to finding out what ought or ought not to be done? Kant answers this question by arguing that 'duty carries with it the necessity to act out of reverence for the law'.[14] It becomes 'categorically imperative' to act in accord with the law once we will that it should become a universal law. Such imperatives are hypothetical only until we will that they should become universal in this way. Once we do this, then duty requires that we conform our actions to them. If we are really moral, moreover, we will do our duty so defined gladly even, and even especially so, when it counts against our inclination or desire. Duties, so defined, become *a priori* duties in the sense that they are defined prior to and independently of any specific applications. By way of example, Kant defended the view that it was immoral to tell a lie under any circumstances.[15] Respect here for truthfulness is placed above respect for life, whenever, for example, the telling of a lie could save a life. This is a much debated claim, but it is entirely consistent with a view, such as Kant's, which places universalizability literally and without exception at the centre of formal ethics.

The influence of Kant, particularly on European Protestant ethics, for example such as those of Barth and Brunner in the twentieth century, has been immense. Whenever intrinsic moral values are discussed the continuing influence of Kant is invariably close at hand. Deontological ethics are, however, largely negative and proscriptive. They are better at telling us what not to do than they are at telling us what to do. Moreover, such ethics are parasitic in the sense that they provide a means only of testing previously arrived at hypotheses. Indeed, it may be suggested that they are socially and politically dangerous in the sense that they leave it open for those that want to manipulate public opinion to change the definition of what duty requires. This is a comparatively easy task if the essence of morality is seen less in what is done and more in the view that whatever is done must be done as a duty. For this reason the possible links between the ethics of Nazism and those of Kant are often noted. However, the possibility that there are intrinsic rights and wrongs which brook no exception is a haunting one; especially in matters of life and death. In Western Christianity it is, principally, the Roman Catholic tradition that offers the view that there are such intrinsic moral values. This has gone with the, perhaps necessary, ecclesiastical system of authority which both defines and imposes intrinsic values. Since the Second Vatican Council, and as a more general result of its opening to external influences, Roman Catholic moral theology is now much wider in outlook and enters into sympathetic dialogue with other claims and influences. Debates on moral issues between, for example, the Catholic and Protestant traditions are now much more open and mutually stimulating than they have ever been.[16] But, for all that, older deontological emphases not infrequently remain and they are important to remember, if for no other reason than that alternative theories of morality also have their limitations and these can often be highlighted by calling to mind deontological objections to them.

Ethical utilitarianism

A central difficulty with understanding morality deontologically arises from its failure to recognize that the morality of our actions must have at least something to do with an assessment of the desirability, or otherwise, of their consequences. The systematic recognition of this is comparatively modern and dates from the eighteenth century. It explicitly argues that the rightness or wrongness of actions is to be ascertained by an assessment of the desirability or otherwise of the consequences to which they give rise. This is why this approach to morality is often called 'consequentialism'. It was originally known as utilitarianism, because of its founder Jeremy Bentham's claim that morality centred on the 'principle of utility'.[17] The view is still known also by this name. The principle of utility was meant as a formal means of enabling us to decide whether or not our actions would lead to desirable ends or otherwise. This approach to moral problem solving has been so influential and popular that none but a very few totally committed deontologists would wish to deny that something like utility is central to morality, if not entirely definitive of it. What follows is a brief account of utilitarianism, with some critical considerations.

The eighteenth-century background to ethical utilitarianism is to be found in a broad movement known as philosophical radicalism. This arose from a concern to subject social, political and economic issues to rational scrutiny. It resulted in a widespread and sustained reforming zeal which was to come to fruition in the great English Reform Bill of 1832. Chief among the early Philosophical Radicals, as they were known, was Jeremy Bentham (1748–1830). In place of what he called *ipsedixitism*, whereby norms of justice were decided on nothing more than the whims of its administrators, he proposed that the principle of utility should become the sole basis for jurisprudence and moral reform. Bentham's doctrine of utility can be studied in his *Introduction to the Principles of Morals and Legislation* (1789), in the opening sentence of which he claims that 'Nature has placed mankind under the governance of two sovereign masters, pain and pleasure.'[18] All attempts to throw off subjection to these two masters are futile.

Such subjection is the foundation of Bentham's system. Pain and pleasure, their very existence and relationship have thus to be seen as protean facts of life. The aim must always be to maximize pleasure and minimize pain. This is precisely, he claims, what the principle of utility enables us to do.

> By the principle of utility is meant that principle which approves or disapproves of every action whatsoever, according to the tendency which it appears to have to augment or diminish the happiness of the party whose interest is in question: or, what is the same thing in other words, to promote or oppose that happiness.[19]

This principle of utility is quite independent of the will of God and can even serve as a test as to whether what claims to be of that will is good or otherwise. Rightness, so understood, attaches to the desirability of the consequences of our actions and is not, therefore, an intrinsic quality at all. This principle can be applied, quite simply, to morality by calculating whether or not the consequences of any particular action would be more beneficial in the sense of promoting more happiness than some other. As a means of achieving this Bentham advocated the use of his 'hedonistic calculus'. This presupposes that pain and pleasure can always be identified and quantified. They both arise from four sources, the first of which is the basis of the following three: physical, political, moral and religious. In considering an instance of pain and pleasure in this way it is necessary to calculate its: intensity, duration, certainty or uncertainty, propinquity or remoteness, its fecundity, purity and chances, if any, of its producing results of an opposite nature. In addition, it is necessary to consider the distribution of such pain and pleasure among those whom it affects. To assist with this Bentham proposed the greatest happiness principle whereby the happiness of the greatest possible number of persons is sought.[20]

The immediate attraction of Bentham's simple proposals is that they take, so to speak, the mystery out of morality by subjecting it to rational calculation. This, for him, was further reaffirmed by what is known as associationist psychology, a means whereby it was thought possible to study the ways ideas are associated (hence the name), and actions determined by them. Claims were made for this which suggest that it appropriated the laws of psychology just as Newton's theories had done for those of physics. Bentham's theories not only had a profound effect on the general ways in which human happiness was actually sought, it prompted a wider debate about the nature of morality which still continues. In an essay on the subject in 1863, 'Utilitarianism', J. S. Mill supported the principle of utility on the grounds that it alone was able to show how moral judgements were a branch of ordinary reason and not, as some Intuitionists and others had formerly claimed, to be sought *via* a special reason or faculty. In response to a widespread criticism of Bentham which claimed that he was mistaken in claiming that all pleasures are equal, 'pushpin is as good as poetry', Mill distinguished the 'higher' from the 'lower' pleasures, but when asked who would be capable of making such a distinction replied only that it would be done by the 'competent judges'.[21] Mill's concession, however, opened an ongoing debate about utilitarianism. His main contribution to it was to focus on the need for the identification of commonly held 'desires' and on identifying the best possible means of securing them. We will now consider some of the fundamental objections to utilitarian theories of morality.

The question is often asked, is the utility of our actions contingent upon the actual or the intended consequences to which they give rise? In other words, can we be held morally responsible for a consequent unacceptable state-of-affairs if we did not intend to bring it about when we acted as we did in good faith? Some who answer 'no' to this also argue that there are unavoidable 'double effects' to many of our actions and these are both good and bad. It is further argued that, provided we did not intend the bad, when we acted as we did, we cannot be held morally responsible for it. An obvious retort to this is to ask how can another person possibly know what our actual intention was when we so acted. Such intention is not open to scrutiny, since the only evidence for it is given by the individual who may be seeking exoneration from moral responsibility. Yet, there must remain a sense in which we cannot be held entirely responsible for all the actual consequences of our actions, since it is frequently difficult to predict in advance what they may be in their entirety. A second major criticism of consequentialist ethics arises from this fact; namely, that they are based on an ever-receding area of uncertainty. Can our moral certainties, it may be asked, be derived from such manifest uncertainty? This criticism of consequentialist ethical theory is a powerful one. Again, it leads to another. What exactly is a 'consequence' of an action? Ethical utilitarians often talk as though consequences are not only predictable in advance, but also that they are in a sense self-contained, as though, once brought about they do not interact with anything else. This is surely not the case. Consequences of actions reverberate and in so doing they frequently change their character. Hence, to act in a certain way is to effect a changed state-of-affairs which itself becomes part of wider reverberating changes as time and events proceed. Clearly, the actual consequences of our actions are more dynamic and less predictable than we often pretend they are when we cite their desirability or otherwise as a reason for advocating the morality of our actions.

Many have defended utilitarian ethical theory from this sort of criticism by distinguishing between 'act' and 'rule' utilitarianism. By the latter, particular moral acts are judged according to whether or not, by general agreement, they would promote happiness according to general expectations.

For all these and other criticisms of ethical utilitarianism we can now scarcely hope to act morally at all unless we contemplate, in some sense, the desirability of the consequences of our actions. But, as we have noted in an earlier discussion, this claim has recently been subjected to a major attack by Alasdair MacIntyre who describes the widespread acceptance of utilitarian ethics as leading to the failure of what he calls the Enlightenment project.[22] In its place, MacIntyre advocates a much older, Aristotelian, approach to moral decision making which takes it as axiomatic that no account of the nature of morality can be arrived at unless it is related to some desirable *telos* or end to which we think all human action should aspire. Morality, he argues, is the business of getting humans from where they are to where, in the light of such an end, we think they ought to be.[23] In this way, MacIntyre is attempting to return the modern understanding of morality to its ancient roots in the classical understanding of virtue. The one he prefers is the Aristotelian, on the grounds that he thinks it to answer correctly questions raised by Plato in *The Republic*.[24] Aristotle, according to MacIntyre, correctly understood the profound sense in which human beings both individually and collectively are bound up with their own narratives in which history and social identity coincide. Such narratives survive in living tradition which is understood as 'an historically extended, socially embodied argument, and an argument precisely in part about the goods which constitute that tradition'.[25] Within such a tradition the pursuit of goods can span generations.

MacIntyre's thesis has received sustained critical attention and has been central to recent debates about morality. He replied to the initial stages of this in the second edition of *After Virtue* published in 1985. One criticism, by Frankena, claimed that MacIntyre was incorrect in supposing that history, however understood, could solve moral confusion. Another pointed out that possession of the virtues would in no way ensure their pursuit. MacIntyre's reply to such is bound up with his preference for the Thomist version of the classical virtues with its emphasis on practical wisdom and the theological virtues of faith, hope and charity. Commenting on this recently, Dorothy Emmet writes:

> I am aware of a considerable philosophical world (contemporary Thomism) going on in its own milieu in virtual isolation from most analytic philosophy. MacIntyre knows analytic philosophy from within. If he can bring its critical methods to bear on contemporary Thomism, it may be possible for others of us to come closer to it. It may also be possible for Thomists to test the resources of their philosophy to meet the demands of a very different intellectual climate from that in which their tradition was formed.[26]

Because, as we shall see, there is now a need to establish an awareness of 'global ethics', MacIntyre's project may well help to recover a sense of the total human narrative in which common goods can be pursued. To the extent in which the rationalist tradition stands outside such a narrative it will be difficult for it to participate. What it does have to offer, however, among other things, is the means of coping with unprecedented novelty in modernity which the older traditions clearly do not. This debate is of central importance to pastoral theology as it seeks to discover the best conditions for human flourishing and, in particular, the requirements within them for collective responsibility and identity.

Natural law

One way in which Christians have tried to discern the will of God in morality is by natural law, which can be traced back to at least the fifth century BCE and is generally taken to mean that by observation of nature and human life it is possible to discern norms, or laws, the keeping of which is in everyone's interest because of our common humanity. Philosophers who have attempted to define natural law, as many have done in the Western tradition, have disagreed over their views of human nature and, therefore, also over their definitions of the laws which can be derived from its observation. However, the principal influence on natural law theory in Western Christianity has been that of Thomas Aquinas.[27] Drawing on the Aristotelian claim that the good life was that lived in accord with nature, Aquinas held that, by reason, it was possible to discover four levels of cosmic reality which manifest themselves in law. They are: eternal law, natural law, divine law and human law.[28] Eternal law is identical with the will of God and natural law is the reflection of that in the created order. Its foundation is in the universal human desire to seek good and avoid evil. Aquinas argued that examples of this are social instincts, the preservation of life, begetting and educating children, seeking truth and developing intelligence. Natural law, so understood, was the name for the participation in the divine law by humans. Such natural laws can change by addition. Aquinas thought that the acceptability of the institution of private property was an example of this.[29] Aquinas' view of natural law was followed by claims, such as those by the so-called 'legal voluntarists' in the sixteenth century, which argued that laws are imposed upon humankind by God rather than discovered by human reason. It was thus held by some that they are revealed in Scripture.

A central difficulty in natural law theory is that of deciding what is 'natural', or more particularly, in deciding *who* decides what is natural. What seems so to one will not necessarily be so to another. For this reason so-called natural laws may often be nothing more than what we might call 'disguised stipulative definitions'. Meaning by that that someone merely stipulates what is natural and presses it upon others thereby pretending it is something that it is not. This is why systems of morality which have drawn heavily on natural law, such as those in the Roman Catholic tradition, have gone with authoritarian systems of morality in which the definition of what is natural can be maintained and enforced. A modern example of this was in the Papal Encyclical *Humanae Vitae* in which it was argued that everyone must keep the rules laid down by natural law, that 'every act of marriage must, in itself stay destined towards the chance of human procreation'.[30] The widespread debate this caused is well-known, but the position is still officially that held by the Roman Catholic Church, although it is reputedly widely ignored by many devout Roman Catholic married couples who are not chastised for it by sympathetic priests. Against the official view, many have held that the use of artificial means of contraception is morally licit on the grounds that it inculcates responsibility and thereby contributes to the sum of human happiness. Debate about the place of natural law theory in Christian ethics continues and this is necessary because of the belief that if the world was created by a loving God it must reflect his loving purposes in some way. For this reason theories of natural law have to be discussed in relation to the doctrine of creation, of which they can be seen as part. The comparative recent neglect of natural law theory in Protestant theology is undoubtedly associated with the equal neglect of the doctrine of creation. A further reason why natural law theory refuses to go away is because it is, by implication, part of an active contemporary and largely secular discussion about human rights, references to which are to be found in the Charter of the United Nations and the Universal Declaration of Human Rights. These documents seek to define human rights in ways which are independent of their definition in different national legislatures. Interestingly, this aim is remarkably similar to that which prompted Cicero's attempt to discover laws which,

> will not be different laws at Rome and at Athens, or different laws now and in the future, but one eternal and unchangeable law will be valid for all nations and for all times, and there will be one master and one ruler, that is God, over us all, for he is the author of this law, its promulgator, and its enforcing judge.[31]

Definitions of human rights are now prominent because they are given front-rank diplomatic status, as they have been at least since the time of President Carter in the USA, since when significant progress has been made in areas where such rights had formerly been denied. They are again being given this status in much current British government foreign policy. The Christian obligation to participate in debates about human rights brings with it also an obligation not to neglect the theological questions it raises and these, again, are in large part those about natural law. In seeking possible answers to such questions it will be enough that we gain some insight into the fundamentals of the human condition and, although this may be much less than strident natural law theorists would like, it will not be insignificant. This mention of the tentative nature of moral enquiry raises an issue to which we must now turn.

The mystery of morality

Debate about the relative merits of different analytic approaches to morality at its best enables us to obtain clearer insights into the essential mystery of moral decision making. The reason for such mystery is not difficult to understand. Recall that the first face of morality that we discussed was the human one. When considering the factual and analytic faces of morality this human face must be kept in mind. Moral problems are frequently very intractable: we do not know how to solve them and even when we claim that we have done so, we may find it difficult to explain why. Clearly, there is something about moral endeavour which often pushes us to the limits of our knowledge and even endurance. Making moral decisions, as we have seen, is part of what it means to be human. This means that in the study of morality we come face to face with the essential mystery of human existence itself, which is why we find it so difficult to explain.

The elements of this mystery have been helpfully described as being like those of light in a prism.[32] At any time it is difficult to discern the hues of light separately because they constantly change their appearance and interaction. No single hue can ever be isolated and used as a total explanation of what light is. All the elements interact and we have to accept the inevitability of their inseparability. In a sense, the use of the analogy of a prism may be taken as a soft way of reconciling serious differences of opinion about morality and, indeed, it could easily become so if we used it to excuse ourselves from the inescapable rigours of analytic enquiry which serious moral endeavour requires. The analogy of the prism helps, however, when after such an enquiry we need a picture to help us keep all the elements of morality in view.

What then, we may again ask, is a 'solution' to a moral problem? For some it can be nothing less than an absolute certainty of some kind or another. But such certainties, desirable though they may be, are frequently impossible to attain. An alternative way of considering the nature of solutions to moral problems is to see them, as Aristotle suggests, as only admitting of such certainty as they are capable of.[33] This might often be much less certainty than we would like, but to pretend otherwise is to pretend also that morality is something that it can never be. When making the most traumatic of moral decisions which affect the well-being of others we are wise to remember that what counts as a solution to a moral problem is, at best, often nothing more than an agreement on how to proceed in difficult circumstances for the time being. As our view of the prism of morality changes, then so it might be necessary to shift our opinion about what is morally right in any given instance. This is not to denigrate morality. Quite the reverse, it is meant to show what a profoundly human thing it is, and to remind us that we are undoubtedly mistaken when we are ever tempted to think otherwise. Those views of morality which will remain most attractive are, for these reasons, those which are capable of change and development. These alone hold out the possibility of us keeping pace with a rapidly changing world in which the alternative of opting out in favour of a long past golden age of certainty is no longer available.

Global ethics

An important example of a recent development in Christian morality is the attention now given to the need to develop a 'global ethics'. This is a response to a previous emphasis, which we have earlier discussed, on the need to develop a global theology. This debate was effectively initiated by Wilfred Cantwell Smith, who stressed that, 'Unless men (*sic*) can learn to understand and to be loyal to each other across religious frontiers, unless we can build a world in which people profoundly of different faiths can live together and work together, then the prospects for our planet's future are not bright.'[34]

Similarly, in a later work Smith writes, 'Our new task is to interpret intellectually the cosmic significance of human life generically, not just for one's own group specifically (let alone, not fail to know or to interpret that significance).'[35]

We have reflected elsewhere on the debate about inter-religious under-standing which arose out of Smith's work and on how it led to a recognition of the importance of a pluralism on a global scale. Christian ethicists have generally welcomed this and, in so doing, have recognized that discrete ethical traditions such as the Judaeo–Christian one can only maintain their integrity if they address global issues and, moreover, do so in collaboration with those who work out of other such traditions. Significant progress with all this has yet to occur. The reason being, in all probability, that the levels of toleration it requires religions to show to each other, as a necessary condition, do not yet exist.[36] Moreover, it is necessary not just that different traditions and groups tolerate each other, they also have to establish levels of genuine understanding as a further precondition to dialogue. Little wonder that progress is so slow.

The term 'global ethics' emerged in the 1990s. The first meeting of the Council of the Parliament of the World's Religions, which met in Chicago in 1993, was seminal. It led to the publication of a Declaration: *A Global Ethic*,[37] the central claim of which is that without such there can be no new world order and that 'The principles expressed in this global ethic can be affirmed by all persons with ethical convictions, whether religiously groun-ded or not.'[38] All this requires that Christianity relinquishes the remarkable position it found itself in at the end of the last century in which, as a legacy of Empire, it had captured a unique position in the world.[39] The social and political forces which resist all this are on a par with the religious ones, as represented by perhaps the majority of Christians who tenaciously cling to a belief in the, however challenged, superiority of their own tradition over all others, religious and secular. An emergent global ethic also faces challenges from secularists who, despairing of the ability of religions to rise to the need, insist that a global ethic must and can only be a secular one. Although secularity will play its part in the wider scene, it cannot do this alone for the simple reason that it is as divided within itself as the religions are and equally bound by its own historic self-interests.

In *Responsibility and Christian Ethics* (1995), William Schweiker replies to the secularist challenge by outlining 'a way of thinking about issues of power, moral identity, and ethical norms by developing a theory of responsibility from a specifically theological viewpoint'. He argues that this will require the transvaluation of values as it aspires to encompass a world view.[40] All this, he adds, will require a global sense of responsibility which crosses the old moral boundaries. Schweiker claims that we discover moral values rather than invent them and this is the basis for grounding them in theology. So understood, the aim of the moral life is to enhance persons before God by enriching the common good. This is an important challenge to the assumption that a global ethic has to be a secular one. Again, however, the very theism it advocates is itself revisionary. It does not favour discrete religious traditions, but, rather, challenges them all to a greater openness.[41]

For all these reasons and more, a new global ethic will have to be a radically revisionary one which leaves no contribution to it untouched or even unaltered. It will, therefore, be a profound catalyst for change. It will also be noticeably task-oriented in the sense that it will have to establish agreed objectives and these will be the overriding priority to which all else will have to give way. There will be no room in any of this for the preservation of self-interest among the contributors. Revision and further revision will be the constant requirement. Clearly, those traditions which will be best able to achieve even a little of all this will be those which have themselves come to terms with constant revisionary activities. Elsewhere we have seen that the Christian tradition has been and needs to remain so revisionary as the faith it professes is made and remade this side of the Kingdom of God.

Yes to a Global Ethic (1996), edited by Hans Küng, is another major contribution. It contains numerous commentaries on the Parliament of the World's Religions' declaration and outlines the establishment of a Global Ethic Foundation in Tubingen which is committed to inter-cultural and inter-religious research, education and encounter.[42] It is yet too early to predict what will come of these initiatives. It is just possible that they are asking too much of discrete religions and ideologies by seeking a utopia in which they can all co-exist. Without wishing to detract at all from that laudable aspiration, in the end all we might realistically expect is that religions and secular ideologies will stay much as they are, but that they will, nonetheless, co-operate in ways we have as yet not seen on such a scale and, in so doing, move closer to the envisaged ideal.

Moral issues in pastoral care

There is one common way in which pastoral care raises moral issues, particularly when it is exercised from a Christian point of view. Christianity is synonymous with moral stances, for reasons we have discussed. These, invariably, purport to be in accord with the will of God and in the best interest of God's creatures. Indeed, reconciling these two factors is, in large part, what Christian moral seriousness is about. It is at the centre of all debates about how Christians and others should act morally, principally because of theological beliefs about the manifestation of God's righteousness in human affairs. But we are seldom certain about what God's righteousness requires in every pastoral instance. This can be a cause of deep conflict between Christian people in which they are not always divided along confessional lines. Such moral confusion among Christians and others is and will remain universal, this side of the Kingdom of God. The foregoing observations about the nature of Christian morality bear particularly on pastoral care. It is here that the human face of morality presents itself most poignantly and it is often just where and why pastors become engaged. The immediate question is, does the Christian pastor bring to every pastoral situation preconceived and non-negotiable moral standards? And is meeting these something the cared-for have to do as a condition of receiving such pastoral ministrations? One way of meeting this problem is to say, as is often said, that the care can be exercised even if it is made necessary by an action or actions which cannot be tolerated.

Care for a convicted murderer would be a moving example of this, as would the care for any person or persons whose need was made necessary by conduct which was thought to be grossly immoral. Care of this kind is frequently necessary, if often in less dramatic circumstances. Its exercise needs to draw on profound theological convictions about the all pervading nature of God's grace and about the hope of the sinner's repentance in the next life if not in this one. Important though it is to make such a distinction between the 'sinner and the sin', it remains of limited assistance, especially when we are comparatively seldom able to be certain about the nature and status of the sin. A great deal of pastoral care, by far its greater part, occurs in situations where the 'sin' is equivocal and where, as a result, the pastor, as well as the pastored, are both in a dilemma about the extent to which either specific actions are sins at all, or if they are, whether they should be tolerated. Brief discussion of two examples of this will illustrate the point.

A homosexual relationship of love may be entered into by persons of devout Christian conviction, some of whom may feel that it is no barrier to them assuming particular responsibilities such as those in Christian ministry. Moreover, they often see no dichotomy at all between the practice of their homosexuality and their Christian spiritual integrity. Indeed, many homosexuals, just as heterosexuals, can be moral, sensitive, caring and effective in their ministrations. Whilst it is possible to take the view that the practice of homosexuality, as distinguished from a homosexual disposition, is totally unacceptable from a Christian point of view, not all take this position. This is a good example of the sort of dilemma we have been discussing. Short of rejecting homosexuality, either punitively or non-punitively, its qualified or non-qualified acceptance is necessary. Such acceptance is now frequently based on the realization that sexual orientation is not a matter of free choice and that we inherit it, rather as we inherit other chromosomal factors about which we can do nothing. Three responses to this are possible and they all accept the disposition of homosexuality as a given. Either (a) total abstinence from the practice of homosexuality is enjoined, or (b) homosexual acts are tolerated as a less than perfect but unavoidably necessary expression of sexuality. If the latter, then lifelong stable relationships are often encouraged. (c) Homosexual relations are treated in exactly the same way as heterosexual relationships and judged by their quality of love. If this view is taken, then it is close to the full acceptance of homosexuality as a given feature of human relationships which finds its place along with others. If this happens, then it may be difficult to deny some homosexuals access to full Christian discipleship including ministry. The pastoral needs thus presented by homosexuals are all too evident and pastors are also required to be particularly sensitive to homophobia, a heterosexual fear of homosexuality and of homosexuals. This is commonly found among those who, for whatever reason, perhaps their own latent sexual ambivalence, reject homosexuality unconditionally and often with an unfeeling harshness which Christians ought not to accept. How, then, do we understand, accept or reject homosexuality from a

Christian point of view? Most of the Christian churches are currently wrestling with this question and, as yet, show little sign of a unanimous approach in their answers to it, beyond the fact that they show at least a willingness to consider the non-punitive acceptance of homosexuality in some form or other.

A similar nexus of pastoral need and endeavour presents itself in the debate about the acceptability or otherwise of remarriage after divorce. Here we meet, again, questions about the Christian acceptability of those who have remarried after divorce and present themselves as candidates for the Christian ministry. Whilst some Christians still believe that an outright prohibition on such remarriage is necessary, perhaps the majority are now uncomfortable with this. As a result, Christian remarriage after divorce is widely available and not considered a bar to those in or entering the ministry. Here, again, there is much contemporary debate in the Christian churches. Experienced pastors will know well how issues such as these are an everyday part of meeting pastoral need.

Dilemmas such as these have been much discussed by the distinguished, but to some controversial, North American pastoral theologian Charles Curran. He observes that contemporary pastoral theology 'can no longer be content to discover the dividing line between sin and no sin'.[43] The reason he gives for this is that pastoral theology and Church authority must follow the experience of Christian people just, he claims, as the Roman Catholic Church did when it moved away from its long-standing condemnation of usury. He sees examples such as this as evidence of the work of the Holy Spirit in human affairs. Acknowledging the need for the sort of provisionality we have discussed, Curran writes, 'The Church at times must speak about particular issues and problems, but teaching on such matters must be somewhat tentative.'[44] As a result, moral theology is being forced to reconsider the existence of absolute universal laws of behaviour which are obligatory in all circumstances. Although Curran writes as a Roman Catholic moral theologian, albeit no longer in an official capacity, what he has to say here is equally applicable to working pastorally out of any Christian tradition, for they all in their own ways grapple with the same need to defend moral standards on the one hand, yet to be mindful of the frequent shortcomings of such standards on the other. What Curran encourages us all to see is that conformity to authoritative pastoral teaching may not always be intrinsically virtuous.

In this final chapter we have seen that pastoral virtue does not always fit easily into conventional categories of philosophical or church dogma. The great strength of Curran's position is his acceptance of the fundamental mysteries which surround human flourishing. Recognizing this requires as much courage of pastors as it does of those they care for. A courage to live with the tensions and uncertainties which create the need to trust in the redeeming power of God's love and grace, as the patient work of pastoral care and concern seeks signs of God's Kingdom amid confusion and even despair. In this there is no place for the easy abandonment of norms and values. What we meet, rather, is the challenge of accepting human need as the mysterious thing it invariably is. Understanding this is what pastoral theology, at its best, aspires to do and it achieves that whenever it meets pastoral need by making and remaking the biblical faith.

Following an introductory consideration of the ordinary nature of pastoral acts we have now proceeded through considerations of how they engage with Christian and secular traditions. Central to all this has been the claim that pastoral care lies at the very heart of the Judaeo-Christian scriptures and the Christian tradition. It is, so understood, the very reason for their existence and for their being as they are. All this is far from considering the pastoral to be something at the fringes of those traditions. It illustrates the importance of considering the anthropological as well as the theological focus of religion. Indeed, the assumption has been made throughout that it is impossible to eliminate anthropology from theology for the simple reason that theology is done by human beings. When they do it, they rise above the human by God's grace to understand something of the redemptive love which God has for his creatures.

Notes

1   See, for example, Kant, I. (1785) *Groundwork of the Metaphysic of Morals*, 1964 reprint. New York: Harper Torchbooks, pp. 61ff.

2   See, for example, Hampshire, S. (1972) *Freedom of Mind and Other Essays*, p. 73. Oxford: Clarendon Press.

3   For an excellent theological discussion of the place of tragedy in the moral life, see Mackinnon, D. M. (1961) *Borderlands of Theology*, pp. 97–104. Cambridge: Cambridge University Press.

4   See Hudson, W. D., ed. (1969) *The Is–Ought Question*, London: Macmillan.

5   Ibid., pp. 130–1.

6   See Hudson, W. D. (1983) *Modern Moral Philosophy*, pp. 1–18. London: Macmillan.

7   Cf. Nygren, A. (1953) *Agape and Eros*, p. 474. London: SPCK.

8   See Preston, R. H. (1981) *Explorations in Theology*, 9, pp. 68–70. London: SCM.

9   Gardner, E. Clinton (1995) *Justice and Christian Ethics*, Cambridge: Cambridge University Press.
10   Ibid., p. 9.
11   See, for example, Finnis, J., Boyle Jr, Joseph M. and Grissez, Germain (1987) *Nuclear Deterrence, Morality and Realism*, pp. 376–8. Oxford: Clarendon Press.
12   Kant, *Groundwork of the Metaphysic of Morals*, p. 61.
13   Ibid., pp. 67–8.
14   Ibid., p. 68.
15   Ibid., pp. 89–90.
16   Cf. Kelly, K. (1966) *Divorce and Second Marriage*, London: Geoffrey Chapman.
17   Bentham, J. (1789) *An Introduction to the Principles of Morals and Legislation*, p. 1. Oxford: Clarendon Press.
18   Ibid., p. 1.
19   Ibid., p. 2.
20   Ibid., p. 1n.
21   Mill, John Stuart, *Utilitarianism*, 1964 reprint of *Utilitarianism, Liberty and Representative Government*, p. 9. London: Everyman's Library.
22   MacIntyre, A. (1981) *After Virtue*, pp. 49–51. London: Duckworth.
23   Ibid., p. 52.
24   MacIntyre, A. (1988) *Whose Justice? What Rationality?*, p. 85. London: Duckworth.
25   MacIntyre, A. (1985) *After Virtue* (second edition), p. 221. London: Duckworth.
26   Emmet, D. (1996) *Philosophers and Friends*, p. 88. London: Macmillan.
27   For a critical discussion see 'Aquinas and the Natural Law', by O'Connor, D. J. in Hudson, W. D. (1974) *New Studies In Ethics*, vol. 1, pp. 79–172. London: Macmillan.
28   Aquinas, St Thomas, *Summa Theologica*, Part II, Q91.
29   Ibid., Part II, Q91, Article 5.
30   Harris, Peter *et. al.* (1968) *On Human Life*, p. 124. London: Burns & Oates.
31   Cicero, *De Republica*, III, xxii, 33; 1995 edition, ed. J. E. G. Zetzel. Cambridge: Cambridge University Press.
32   Emmet, D. (1979) *The Moral Prism*, London: Macmillan.
33   Aristotle, *Ethics*, BKI ch. 3; 1955 edition. Harmondsworth: Penguin Classics, pp. 27–8.
34   Cantwell Smith, W. (1978) *The Meaning and End of Religion*, p. 8. London: SPCK.
35   Cantwell Smith, W. (1981) *Towards a World Theology*, pp. 186–7. London: Macmillan.
36   See p. 42 above.
37   Küng, Hans and Kuschel, Karl-Josef, eds (1993) *A Global Ethic*, London: SCM.
38   Ibid., p. 19.
39   Ibid., p. 82.

40   Schweiker, William (1995) *Responsibility and Christian Ethics*, p. 30.
     Cambridge: Cambridge University Press.
41   For an extended discussion of the theological implications see Markham, Ian
     S. (1994) *Plurality and Christian Ethics*, Cambridge: Cambridge University
     Press.
42   Küng, H. (1996) *Yes to a Global Ethic*. London: SCM.
43   Curran, C. E. (1968) *A New Look at Christian Morality*, p. 73. Notre Dame,
     Indiana: Fides Publishers.
44   Ibid., p. 98.

Conclusion

This has been a long journey from the initial reflections on Charles Causley's sixth hospital visitor. In it a variety of themes have become intertwined. The first and main theme has been the location of the pastoral, (that is, care for others), at the heart of all Christian theological reflection and, along with that, the rejection of the widespread view that the pastoral is but an application of a theology which is separately constructed for other reasons. This understanding of the pastoral nature of theology itself lies consistently at the heart of the Old and New Testaments. Indeed, the claim was made that the Bible yields to fresh insight when it is read in this way. This was the heart of the biblical faith. That faith is still in the making, in the sense that its living out in subsequent Christian history and the present is a continuation of the dynamic creativity of the biblical life. It focuses on human identity, in the sense that it confronts us powerfully with questions about how humans are understood in relation to the manner and purpose of their existence. The Christian understanding of that identity was explored in comparison and dialogue with others which have prevailed influentially in the twentieth century.

There followed examples of how the pastoral, so understood, motivated examples of the greatest thinkers of the Church: Augustine, the Protestant Reformers and Karl Barth. They were all faced with the monumental task of having to reconstruct theology and the life of faith in the face of a collapse, or the collapsing, of what had gone immediately before. Here again, there were remarkable resonances with the way the faith was pastorally made and remade throughout biblical history.

The second theme necessarily emerges from the first: the past and present need to be in conversation. The past is a problem: how can it in all its strangeness and often seeming inaccessibility relate to the present at all? Here archaism was rejected on the one hand and presentism rejected on the other, preferring, instead, a model of the relationship between the two which saw them in constant 'conversation'. This model allowed for and required both the constant re-mining of the past and cognizance of modernity however novel it may be. This was seen as the milieu in which the faith of the Bible and Christian history is continuously lived out in the present. It is what gives it its freshness as well, as it prepares us for the awesome tasks which the continuing life of faith requires. Examples of these were given throughout the discussion. All this is in very stark contrast to an understanding of that life which supposes that it requires only that we live in the cipher of what others have done before us, especially those in the biblical dispensation. How odd that it can be thought at all that this is what is required of us, when it manifestly never occurred to the biblical writers that this was only what was required of them. They went on making and remaking the biblical faith in its intrinsically pastoral dimension and so must we. The brief insight into the way St Paul wrestled with tradition and modernity in the face of ever-changing pastoral needs, provided a profound paradigm of what the pastoral life requires of us all.

The third theme considered the traditional pastoral agenda, the care of individuals. The reasons why and the way in which the care of individuals has been prominent in the Protestant churches was considered. Important though that remains, it was then shown that much contemporary psychoanalysis and therapy rests on anthropological assumptions which are unacceptable from a Christian point of view. It was then shown why it is necessary to broaden the notion of care for individuals into the wider sphere of care for societies. In passing, throughout these discussions some central topics illustrated how the earlier central themes of the book, described above, worked themselves out in the present. This theme concluded with a chapter on pastoral care and morality. Here again, the biblical faith was seen to be constantly made and remade in the continuing confrontation with modernity and the challenge all that brings to the conjunction of the pastoral and moral life.

All this is the stuff of the Christian pastoral life and of its heart in the ever ongoing theological remaking which is required by a living faith. It demands, as we have seen throughout, that we be open to modernity and also be steeped in understanding our own tradition, its theology, spirituality and, it must importantly be remembered, the rituals of prayer and worship which sustain it. It is here that pastoral care and theology shade into one to become part of the complete Christian life.

Name index

Subject index

morality   chapter 7 *passim*,   21–2, 130–1
    consequentialism and   156–60
    deontology and   154–6
    'faces' of   146–50
    pastoral acre and   166–9
    prism model and   22, 163
    private/public   133–5
    'second order'   149–50
    war and   101–2, 148

natural law   160–2
Nazism   36, 120, 129, 140, 155
nuclear weapons   *see* peace

pastoral actions   22
pastoral theology
    culture and   83–9
    definitions of   2–4, 126–7, 146
    lost identity   81–2
    politics and   34
    St Paul and   5, 63, 67–74, 173
    traditional theology and   4–8
peace   97–102
    just war and   99–102
    nuclear weapons and   100–2, 140–1, 148
    see also Jesus
penultimate questions   xi
pluralism   21–2, 42, 44, 153
political realism   141
    Niebuhr on   135–8
positivism   30, 37–8
    behaviourism and   37–8

psychotherapy   82, 107–12, 173
    existentialism and   118–21
    Freud and   100–12, 117–18
    see also counselling

redaction criticism   56
reformation   47, 74, 77, 84, 92, 104–7, 124, 128–9

self-help   110
sexuality   31–2
    homosexuality   122, 167–8
    psychotherapy and   110–11, 122
sin
    Niebuhr on   95–7
social ethics   80, 127
sociology of knowledge   75

theology
    dialectical   16
    historical   74–7
    political   128–9
    praxis and   17
    pure/applied   5, 16–18
    social   127–33
    two kingdoms and   14
    see pastoral

utilitarianism   145, 156–60
    see also morality

war   *see* peace